COLLECTOR'S ENCYCLOPEDIA of

POTTERY

VOLUME 2

REVISED EDITION

SHARON & BOB HUXFORD
and
MIKE NICKEL

On the front cover:
Olympic vase, Persia and Ionia Yoked to the
Chariot of Xerxes, 14½", $7,500.00 – $8,500.00.
(From the collection of Bill Barnett and Terry Moore)

On the back cover:
Mara vase, 8", with ceramic seal and chevron, $6,000.00 – $7,000.00.
(From the collection of Bill Barnett and Terry Moore)

Cover design by Beth Summers
Book design by Karen Smith

Collector Books
P.O. Box 3009
Paducah, Kentucky 42002-3009

www.collectorbooks.com

Contents

Jardiniere and Pedestal, Luffa, 30", $2,500.00 – 3,000.00.

Dedication

To Allison, our own children, Marka, Michael, and Steven,
and our grandchildren, Amanda, Samantha, Nicole, Mallori, Michael, and Lindsay.

"Not to know what happened before you were born is to be forever a child."
– Cicero

Foreword

These books were originally published in the 1970s, the second edition following the first by four years. During those four years, we were able to do further research and felt we had significant new material to offer. We had discovered some new lines and had become acquainted with many Roseville collectors who had prime examples they were willing to have photographed. So this book was prepared as a companion to the first book — please refer to Volume 1 for the history of the company, as well as a complete listing of lines of production along with descriptions and approximate dates of introduction.

In this edition, you'll see some of the best examples of the early art ware ever produced and a fine representation of Middle Period lines such as Futura, Imperial II, and Pine Cone, to name but a few. We've also identified a new line of Roseville which we have dubbed Cameo II.

Jardinieres and pedestals and umbrella stands are always desirable — several pages are devoted to them, and wall pocket collectors will find that more than one hundred forty are shown in the color plates.

As collectors have become better informed about the Roseville lines, preferences for colors have emerged; this has influenced the market to a great extent, so we are happy to be able to offer a breakdown in our pricing structure where it is needed to reflect these trends.

It has been our pleasure to prepare this book for those who love Roseville..."beauty that never fades."

Wincraft, Dealer Sign, 4½" x 8", $4,000.00 – 4,500.00.

✧ Acknowledgments ✧

These are the acknowledgments as they appeared in the original publication in the 1970s. Though some of the people whose names we mentioned are now deceased, we have made no attempt to take out their names; to do so would suggest that we are not grateful for their kind assistance so many years ago, and that certainly is not the case. Their contributions are still a part of this book.

❖How difficult it is to find adequate measures to express our deep appreciation to the many fine people who have helped us make Volume 2 a reality. With each new undertaking we find an increasing number of interested, supportive people willing to contribute their pottery and their knowledge toward making our book a success. We sincerely thank each one of you.

We want to acknowledge a special indebtedness to Bill Klutts, Connie Westgate, Mike Nickel, and Debbie Reese for the kind hospitality shown to our entire crew during photography sessions that were often disruptive, lengthy, and exhausting. Your kindness and generosity will never be forgotten.

To Ruth and Harold Nichols, Faydell and Sam Schott — all made very long trips to bring fine examples of rare pottery to be photographed.

To Dr. Joseph D. Ferrara and Gerard Leduc of Fer-Duc Inc., Newburgh, N.Y.; M.R. Pedotto; Terry Ford; Rilda and Stan Webb; Bea and Hal Moore; Brenda Roberts; Rose and Ervin Sowards; Maxine Ferguson, Wayside Antiques, Zanesville, Ohio; Norma and Wilson Woods; Kathy and Dan DeVol; John Ketcham; Donna and Max Hazzard; Richard Keiler; Lyle Loux; Betty Adams; Betty and Herbert Ward, Stagecoach Antiques, Zanesville, Ohio; Louise Purviance; Mr. and Mrs. Tom Sawyer; Thelma and Ed Newman; Bobbie and Jim Curry; Robert Campbell; Fadyne and Clarence Carlson and their photographer, Roger L. Waggoner, Ft. Worth, Texas; Mark Koeling; and Si Lambert, Lambert Antiques, Jackson, Ohio.

"Thank you all, so much, for each contribution!"

To two fine people who are by now "regulars" on our crew — our photographer, Ted Wright of Zanesville, and Betty Blair, Zanes Trace Antiques, Zanesville, our "collaborator and co-ordinator" — we send our love, and to Paul, whose presence was appreciated. We're glad you came!

Again, we want to thank Arlene Peterson, Reference Librarian, and the staff of the Ohio Historical Society Archives for their courteous assistance.

To Mom and Dad, Mr. and Mrs. Ray Newnum, and to Bob's mother, Ruth, who sat with our house, our cats, and our young adults, we send much love.❖

We're very grateful to Bill Barnett and Terry Moore who provided us with some wonderful photographs of rarities from their collection — the Home Art urn on the back cover of Volume 1 as well as both pieces shown on the covers of Volume 2. Our thanks to Bill and Kelley Shields and Jerry and Joyce Jackson who provided the Cameo II items from their collections to photograph, putting to rest the identity of a line of pottery that has been a mystery to us all for many years.

About the Authors

After writing their first book, *The Story of Fiesta* published in 1974 (now in its 9th edition) the Huxfords became pottery editors for Collector Books and in that capacity wrote several other books on various Ohio potteries. The *Collector's Encyclopedia of Roseville Pottery* and the *Collector's Catalog of Early Roseville Pottery* were published in 1976; new releases in 1978 included the *Collector's Encyclopedia of McCoy Pottery,* the *Collector's Encyclopedia of Brush-McCoy Pottery,* and the *Collector's Catalog of Brush-McCoy Pottery.* The *Collector's Encyclopedia of Weller Pottery* was published in 1979, and in 1980 they wrote the *Collector's Encyclopedia of Roseville Pottery, Volume II.* Since 1982 they have been editors of *Schroeder's Antiques Price Guide; Schroeder's Collectible Toys, Antique to Modern;* the *Garage Sale and Flea Market Annual,* and *Wanted To Buy.*

Michael (Mike) Nickel is one of the country's best known authorities on Roseville Pottery. Since 1970 he has been not only an avid collector but also a dealer, specializing in the finest examples available. Many pieces from his collection are featured in Volume II. He has again contributed to this edition, and we are happy to be able to offer our readers much more in-depth information than ever before, due entirely to his efforts. Shape numbers have been added whenever possible, the pricing structure (where important) has been broken down by color, corrections have been made to the text to reflect new information that has come to light since our earlier research, and values have been updated to more accurately represent current market activity.

Woodland, Vase, 19", $5,000.00 – 6,000.00.

Mike is a retired advertising creative director and is a former officer of the American Art Pottery Association, having the distinction of holding the Life Member Number One Membership in that organization. He is married to Cynthia (Cindy) Horvath, and together they have written *Kay Finch Ceramics, Her Enchanted World.* They are full-time antiques dealers and travel the circuit extensively. He welcomes comments, questions, and inquiries from readers.

Mike Nickel, PO Box 456, Portland, MI 48875;
(517) 647-7646. Buy, Sell, Appraise.
e-mail: mike5c@voyager.net

Summary in Retrospect

Art Ware to Commercial Lines

In the early days of the Roseville Pottery Company, distribution of their wares was sometimes accomplished by peddlers who regularly made their rounds, hauling assorted goods from door to door, eking out their sustenance by providing the housewife with everyday necessities and an occasional trinket. Before their main office was moved from Roseville to Zanesville in 1898, the company promoted a package deal — a sampling of their wares — which they referred to in their advertisements as the "Canvassers Outfit." (The ad copy is printed in part in the color section.) From the assorted wares they offered, we can learn a little more concerning the type of pottery they produced prior to the turn of the century. A miniature cuspidor and umbrella stand were offered "finished in blended colors, artistically decorated, represent(ing) exactly full size ware." No doubt this blended ware represented a goodly part of their production. Catalogs printed a few years later indicate the retail prices for some of these early blended glazed pieces — the stork umbrella stand, $1.25; some of the mid-price jardinieres and pedestals, $4.00–6.00; and one 45" tall jardiniere and pedestal with female heads sold for $15.00–20.00. Although none of this pre-1900 blended ware was marked, be aware of the shape numbers: jardinieres carry numbers 400 through 499; pedestals, 500 through 599; cuspidors, 600 through 699; and umbrella stands, 700 through 799. Also in the ad, a miniature cooking crock "too well known to need comment" was listed as #315; the salesman's sample Venetian crock on page 47 was probably one of these, marked with a three digit number on the base; the first is 3, the others are not clear.

Roseville began the production of art pottery in their Zanesville plant in 1900. The lovely brown-glazed Rozane is familiar to all Roseville collectors, and the Rozane Light, introduced in 1905, although by no means as plentiful, is nearly always represented by at least one example in almost any serious collection. There are other variations within the line, however, that are extremely scarce. Two types shown in the color plates are, by reason of their unique coloring, very rare and exciting! One is done in a monochromatic palette of soft brown. The other has blended background effects that almost exactly duplicate Weller's Aurelian line — gold and orange streaking is deftly worked in with the dark brown to produce a striking backdrop for the vivid, natural hues of the painting. (Rozane shapes are often elaborate, yet just as often very simple. Shape numbers begin at 800 and run to 999. A small piece of Rozane could be bought for as little as $5.00; the large floor vases were as high as $90.00.)

In the early years of the century until as late as 1920, almost any pottery company in the area manufactured a matt green line. Roseville's first green line in 1904 was called Chloron. In 1905 their Rozane Egypto line was introduced, and it was followed a few years later with another, called simply Matt Green. Collectors have tried to devise an identification process that would separate unmarked Chloron from Egypto by associating the various glaze characteristics with one particular line. Careful comparison of marked examples shows no distinction. *It is the accepted criteria today that to qualify as Egypto, all pieces must bear the Rozane seal.*

Rozane Mara, introduced in 1905, was Roseville's answer to the famous Sicardo line by the S. A. Weller Pottery. Today Mara is much rarer than Sicardo and is almost never marked. Three variations of the lustre glaze are shown in the color plates — each very distinct. In one, the intricate pattern is in sharp contrast to the red lustre background; in a second, the design is very subtle and tends to blend into the overall color. The third and most desirable glaze is brilliant magenta with highlighted areas of metallic lustre over a shape modeled in low relief.

One of the most famous of these early art ware lines was Della Robbia. The 1905 Rozane catalog shows vases, urns, tankards, and bowls in sgraffito decorations with colorful enamels, shapes with dramatic styling, often with reticulated rims. Close observation of later catalogs reveals a completely remodeled line. No handles, no reticulation, less quality and impact in the designs — all signs of the onset of mass production.

This may also explain the fact that many pieces of Rozane Crystalis are found on simple Rozane shapes, rather than those futuristic, almost space-age shapes shown in the 1905 catalog. Two schools of thought exist concerning the evaluation of Rozane Crystalis. Collectors of crystaline glazes judge the quality of the crystals within the glaze. Others prefer the old Crystalis shapes over the more simple Rozane ones.

With little information available concerning the early line called Special in the Roseville catalogs, the answers to some of our questions may never be found. Was this ware decorated by Roseville, or were their shapes decorated by another company and finally sold through Roseville's own catalogs?

Rozane Catalogs in Review

To the collector who has developed a sincere appreciation for the quality of workmanship and the careful attention to detail so apparent in the Roseville product, any type of related material is a coveted treasure — especially such an item as one of the very early Rozane Ware catalogs. Due to the fact that a vast majority of these promotional pamphlets were laid aside, forgotten, and eventually discarded, the number of them that have survived the past 75 years is very small, indeed, and they are considered quite rare. Because many collectors may never have the opportunity to see one of these for themselves, the following articles have been selected from two of these booklets — one is dated 1905.

→ How Rozane Originated ←

Many collectors have asked how we came to make Rozane. It was like this: A certain well-known artist whose special delight was the painting of flowers, sat one evening before a half-finished canvas, intently poring, by the last fading rays of daylight, over a book. At last, sighing, he looked up at his canvas across which reflections of the sunset were cast, mingled with deep shadows.

"Too bad, too bad," said the voice of a stranger, who had been drinking in the charm of the scene.

"You startled me," said the artist, turning, "but listen to this," and he lighted a candle while he read, never thinking to ask who the stranger might be. "It is Ruskin I was reading. Mentioning the permanency of ceramic works as compared with those of other branches of art, he says:

It is surely a severe lesson to us that the best works of Turner could not be shown for six months without being destroyed. I have hope of one day interesting you greatly in the study of the arts of moulding and painting porcelain; and of turning the attention of the workmen of Italy from the vulgar perishable mosaic to the exquisite subtleties of form and color possible in the perfectly docile and afterward imperishable clay. And one of the ultimate results of such craftsmanship might be the production of pictures as brilliant as painted glass — as delicate as the most subtle water colors, and more permanent than the Pyramids.

"I was only thinking, when you spoke, what a shame it is that these efforts of mine have to go the way of Turner's. I'd like to try my hand at the clay."

It reads like a romance, but just here began the Rozane idea of reproducing in art pottery fine productions in oils. The stranger, it chanced, was a skilled potter, then engaged in making models for our less expensive potteries. He set aside a laboratory for experiments and so successful was he that, with the aid of his new-found collaborator, the artist, the soft and natural tints of nature were not only transmitted to the clay but preserved, practically unaltered, even through the intense firing to which the ware is subjected.

The natural tendencies of the Ohio clays run to golden browns and yellows, and these tones, artistically blended, formed the body and background of the first Rozane and are retained in all designs of this first style, now called Rozane Royal, to distinguish it from the new varieties constantly being designed in our studios.

With permanence in art as the prime motive, the first attempts in Rozane have resulted in the organization of a company of artists attracted by the worthy object which prompted the first experiments. These artists are all earnest students in ceramics and all have ideas of their own which they are anxious to work out. The spirit of experiment always prevails in our studios and laboratories. Moreover, each artist has his or her own style and no design is ever duplicated. This accounts for the wide variety of subjects and the strong individuality found in Rozane.

Holding up an ideal for the perfect pottery, a well-known authority on ceramics says: "Let us suppose that a piece of pottery has been painted, and that the action of the fire has made the coloring perennial, so that we find in it a design as everlasting as the ware itself. Let us suppose, further, that the tints are natural, that, in short, the design is all that it should be, and that in the painting, nature is displayed as on the canvas — then we would have a specimen of the perfect union of the potter's and of the painter's art."

This is ROZANE ROYAL.

The Story of Rozane

... from an early Rozane Ware catalog

Upon the edge of the picturesque city of Zanesville, Ohio, stand the plants of the Roseville Pottery Company where the famous Rozane Ware is conceived and executed.

How Rozane Ware differs from other wares, how it acquires that certain something which makes it a distinctive art creation appealing universally to connoisseurs, can perhaps be best explained by an imaginary "little journey" through the plants.

The logical starting point of such an expedition would be the modeling and designing rooms, where artists, carefully selected for their creative ability, are constantly engaged in the evolution of new and graceful patterns.

In one corner stands the old-time potter's wheel, made famous by story and song, on which the material, under the modeler's skillful touch, gathers grace and takes on the faultless symmetry that must characterize every line of every piece created.

None of the hurly-burly of commercialism invades this sanctum of art. The modeler lingers long and earnestly over each piece, taking his own chosen time, often working for days, and even weeks, on a delicately turned bit of ware.

No pattern leaves this room until it has passed the critical eye of the master-artist, for nothing short of the highest degree of excellence may bear the Rozane mark.

After the pattern is completed, a cast of it is made from which subsequent molds are produced. The clay, which comes from the neighboring hills and which is of a particularly desirable quality, is prepared for use by grinding in what is known as a "blunger" mill, after which it is passed through a fine screen, ensuring a smooth and equal consistency. Water is added until a slip of the proper thickness is formed, and it is then ready to pour into the molds which reproduce the various patterns.

It is here that a nice bit of skill and judgment is required. The mold is filled entirely with the thin slip, which immediately begins to adhere to the sides of the mold and to harden. The workman, at just the proper moment, empties the mold of the liquid that is in the center, leaving only sufficient clay adhering to the sides to form the requisite thickness of the vase or whatever the piece may be. The mold is left in a steam-drying room for twenty-four hours; afterward the piece is removed, carefully sponged to ensure perfect smoothness, the handle (if handle there be), is attached, and the piece is ready for blending.

The last few steps have been purely mechanical. We are now in the domain of art again. Before being turned over to the blender, each piece, at this stage, is subjected to a critical examination. If it shows even the most minute imperfection, back it goes to the grinder — that is the Rozane way.

The blending is done by compressed air brushes. Perhaps in this blending, as much as in any other part of the production, is the individual artistic quality of Rozane Ware attained. It is not a mere spraying of color upon color, but the delicate harmonizing of tints and tones, of velvety shadows and shimmering high-lights — a true conception of coloring by artists who feel and know.

The newly blended pieces are kept in the moist atmosphere of the "damp-room" until their turn comes in the finishing room where they are hand-decorated by painters carefully chosen for skill and intelligence. Whether the decoration be a spray of roses or a sprig of ferns, a collection of poppies or a cluster of autumn leaves, the warmth of coloring and fidelity of execution prove the splendid efficiency of the staff of decorators. Many of these decorators are graduates of the great European art schools; others are from the most efficient American institutions — thus embracing the best foreign and native talent.

The colors are applied with artists' ordinary sable brushes. After the decorations are completed, Rozane Ware is ready for the "test of fire," the last step in the manufacturing process.

Again encased in protecting molds, the pieces are placed in immense kilns, where they are subjected to the fierce heat of 1800 degrees Fahrenheit. After the first "firing," they are plunged into a solution of glaze, which not only gives them their beautiful gloss, but makes the decorations permanent. Then they are given a final "firing," and Rozane Ware, in all its beauty and brilliancy, is ready for the market, to gladden the artistic eye and add to the tasteful ornamentation of the most luxuriously appointed homes.

Synopsis of Company Price List, 1916

Floor Vase, DECORATED MATT, 20", #724, (artist's cipher unknown), $7,000.00 – 8,000.00.

In the Roseville files at the Ohio Historical Society, there is a price list dated July, 1916. It is 24 pages long, and full of both enlightening facts and puzzling references.

Alphabetically beginning with "Art," the index refers us to a page entitled "Special Art Assortment." Listed are such familiar things as Matt Green gates, Goodnight candlesticks, Dutch teapots, etc. Sylvan flower vases are listed, two years earlier than we once thought they were produced. "Green Tint" gates are offered, and "Coral" ferns and "Cremona" tobacco jars hint at lines as yet unidentified. (Another page of the catalog is devoted entirely to "Cremona" — tankard sets, smoker sets, dresser sets, and tea sets are listed — and that, along with the fact that during these middle teen years creamware was extremely popular, would strongly suggest that this Cremona was a creamware line. The more familiar Cremona line would not be produced for nearly a dozen more years!)

Birds and bowls were offered in red, blue, black, yellow, carnelian, and matt white, and some birds were available decorated by hand. Bowls were listed in 6", 8", 10", 12", and 14" sizes. Evidently a popular color combination, black bowls were paired with yellow birds, yellow bowls with black birds — sixteen sizes and combinations, all black and yellow, with prices ranging from $10.50 to $22.00 per dozen! Bouquet holders in the shapes of a frog, turtle, fish, and toad were mentioned, finished in the same colors.

Under "Baby Plates" is a nursery assortment of familiar items — bread and milk sets, custards, teapots, etc. — but the bottom half of the page is devoted to the "Holly" line, and reveals that creamers, children's mugs, fern dishes, ashtrays, dresser sets, and smoker sets were produced, in addition to those items we were able to photograph for the color plates.

"Lily of the Valley" was the name of a 12-pc. toilet set — "Osiris" was another. "Jeanette" was offered in cuspidor #909 shape, and later in jardinieres and pedestals and umbrella stands.

"Hoster Flagon Steins" in 8-oz., 10-oz., and 12-oz. sizes were advertised as having a "White lining." Bedroom sets consisting of candlesticks, match receiver, pitcher, and tray, came with either orange or blue bands — there are examples of these in the color plates.

A notation concerning the company policy for pricing tea sets and individual pieces seems sound yet today: Teapot — ½ price entire set; Sugar bowl — ⅓ price entire set; creamer — ½ price of sugar bowl.

And, yes, wall pocket collectors, a Tourist wall pocket is listed — 10" x 5" at $9.00 per dozen! Tourist window boxes are priced at $3.00 for a 6½" x 11", and $4.50 each for 8" x 14". An 8½" x 16" size was offered at $6.00.

The Blended Glazes and Matt Green were popular finishes as were Carnelian, Black, Yellow, and Blue Rosecraft. One was referred to simply as "red." "Red" jardinieres and pedestals in 29" and 33" heights were priced at $4.50 and $7.50 each. These were also offered in the Rosecraft glazes!

So, though informative and exciting, the 1916 price list leaves us with only vague suggestions of a line called "Coral"... a "Cremona"... "Osiris"... a puzzling red glaze ... birds and bowls. Perhaps in the future, further research will give us these answers.

Production After 1917

In 1917 the company was producing a line of utility ware "for hotels, cafés, and family." Romafin was plain and undecorated, in "mahogany red with a white lining." The catalog presented nine pages of the ware in a wide variety of baking pans, pudding crocks, etc. Also listed was a complete line of teapot shapes, some of which were made in a black glaze as well as the mahogany.

"Donatella" tea sets were made in various patterns during this period; included were Ceramic, Dutch, and Landscape. The three-piece sets were priced at $1.25. Seven-piece stein sets in the Dutch pattern sold at $3.00, others were $4.00.

Victorian Art Pottery is a seldom-seen line that was made from 1924 until about 1928. Shapes were simple and there was a selection of three banded designs for the customer to choose from: grapevines and leaves, scarabs, and sailing ships (which is scarce today). Background colors were nearly always standard — blue-gray for the grapevines, brown for the scarabs — though they could be otherwise tailored to accommodate customer preference. On occasion, yellow backgrounds were used as well. (See the color plates for examples.)

By the late '20s and into the early '30s, simple, beautiful glazes were often favored over elaborate modeling. The Futura line combined the best of both the modeler's art and the chemist's technology. Several pages were featured in the company's catalogs. In fact, several Futura shapes were reintroduced in the late 1930s in lines such as Tourmaline, Carnelian II, Ivory, and Artcraft.

In 1926 Russell T. Young, son of George Young, founder of the Roseville Pottery, who was at that time president of the company, built a home at 1327 Blue Avenue in Zanesville. The Tudor-manor style structure was designed by Insco Associates of Columbus, Ohio, and constructed by the Dunzweiler Company. One of the specially designed ceramic tile radiator covers from the home is shown in the color plates. It is from a set designed by Frank Ferrell and made by George Krause.

From as early as 1917, lines that featured a floral pattern were popular sellers. Mock Orange in 1950 ended Roseville's love affair with florals. By the late 1940s in an attempt to revive lagging sales, several lines were produced in a high gloss glaze — however, all met with only limited success.

Our study has only fortified our appreciation for the integrity of the man who founded the Roseville Pottery ... for those that followed and carried on in the same irreproachable manner ... and for the pride taken in their work by the artists and craftsmen who were so dedicated to their art.

Important Notice About Pricing

Prices are based on first-quality pottery in mint condition and represent the high end of average retail. *Mint* herein is defined as having no incurred damage such as chips, hairlines, glaze flaking or staining. Certain factory flaws may also decrease the value of a piece, such as glazed-over chips; pieces not truly molded, leaning or otherwise slightly irregular; poorly finished mold lines; faint embossing; poor color or careless decoration. *Crazing* is the fine network of tiny lines caused by uneven expansion and contraction between body and glaze. You can expect to find it to some extent on items from any production period and in moderate amounts should not affect value. A properly restored item (with an invisible mend) may sell for 60% to 70% of mint value, depending on the extent of restoration.

In earlier lines, the presence of a round Rozane seal (ceramic wafer) or the seal with the attached chevron containing the line name will add at least 25% to our values, possibly even more, especially on these lines: Mara, Mongol, and Crystalis. If there is evidence that a seal/wafer has been removed or shows mutilation, this indicates a factory second that was sold only through their factory outlet on Highway 40. On the early handpainted lines, prices are also based on the quality of the painting, the subject, and the artist who did the painting. Generally speaking, the value of the subject (from highest to lowest) is: complex scenes (which may include people, animals birds or flowers); portraits of people; portraits of animals or birds (dogs being the most common); and finally, floral sprays. Artists' ciphers or signatures add value, at least 20%. And certain artists, among them Mae Timberlake, Hester Pillsbury, Claude Leffler, Fred Steele, Arthur Williams, Walter Myers, John Herold, and Frederick Rhead, command even higher values, which are reflected in the examples pictured on the following pages.

See the index in the back of this book for approximate dates of line introduction; more extensive information of this nature is provided in Volume 1.

Roseville Artists and Their Signatures

Some of the artists whose ciphers are illustrated below and on the following pages are known to have decorated for companies other than Roseville since they were under no exclusive contract there but instead worked free-lance among other area potteries.

Elizabeth Ayers

Virginia Adams
(or full last name)

C. B. (unknown)
Crocus

E. B., E. R. B. (unknown)
Della Robbia

F. B., F. A. B. (unknown)
Della Robbia

G. B. (unknown)
Della Robbia

M. B.

A.F. Best

Jenny Burgoon

E. C. (unknown)
Della Robbia

Charles Chilcote

Dibowski – no signature available

Anthony Dunlavy

Charles Duvall – no signature available

Katy Duvall
Della Robbia

M. F.

Artist	Signature
Gazo Fudji	Fujiyama
Gussie Gerwick	G; G Gerwick
Golde Della Robbia	-G- -Golde-
Madge Hurst	MH.
William Hall Rozane	W.H.
John Herold	J. H.
Josephine Imlay	J.I.; J Imlay
Harry Larzelere	HL

Artist	Signature
Claude Leffler Azurean, Rozane	CL CLL
F. M.	F. M.
L. McGrath – no signature available	
Mignon Martineau	MM
C. Mitchell Rozane	C MITCHELL
Lily Mitchell	LM ; Mitchell
B. Myers	B. MYERS
Walter Myers	W. MYERS

M. N. (unknown)
Rozane

C. Neff
Rozane
(several Neff signatures began with the letter C)

Grace Neff

Mary Pierce

Hester Pillsbury

Frederick H. Rhead

Harry Rhead

Lois Rhead – no signature available

Helen Smith

Fred Steel

C.S. (unknown)
Decorated Matt

E. T. (unknown)
Woodland

Mae Timberlake

Arthur Williams

Roseville's Trademarks

After 1900 when the Rozane art line was added to the commercial wares already in production, the company established a system of identification using a number code. Each series of numbers indicated the particular type of ware being produced, and each number within the series represented a shape. After 1904, though this complicated system was still intact, these numbers did not physically appear on the ware. The practice resurfaced in the mid-'30s, when the cast indented (impressed) mark was adapted for use. There were, however, exceptions during that time. Letters or numbers in ink (usually underglaze) are sometimes found on the bottoms of the commercial art lines of the teens, '20s, and '30s. Certain Donatello and Vista shapes have been found numbered in blue on the bottom (indicative of shape and size), but this is infrequent. Green Tint occasionally carries a crudely impressed number. Later lines beginning with the 1920s and continuing into the mid-'30s carried 3-digit numbers applied with red crayon, but these could easily be removed by washing or cleaning. Other ink markings found on many pieces identified workers who did specialized jobs such as molding, cleaning, decorating, or inspection. These were simply aids to quality control. Pieces with trial glazes were numbered in blue ink, but not under the glaze.

A wide variety of marks were used at the Roseville Pottery. Although some lines were marked in more than one manner, often the mark can be an important factor to consider where proper identification of a line is in question, i.e., a novice could distinguish Florane (which carries mark #11) from the 1940s Rozane (mark #19) simply by observing the mark. As he becomes more familiar with the pottery, he would recognize either line by shape or by the slight color variations. Similarly, while both Panel and Silhouette have a few shapes that are decorated with nude panels, even before a beginning collector learns to recognize their distinctive colors and shapes, by simply looking at the marks the line identification is obvious, since Panel is marked Rv (#11) and Silhouette Roseville, U.S.A., in relief (mark #19).

The dates given for the marks below indicate the period of greatest use; however, it is generally felt that the use of some marks extended beyond the time that a new one was developed.

MARK 1

ROZANE
RPCo

RPCo

Die impressed mark used from 1900 – 1904.

MARK 2

Paper sticker, ca. 1900, very rare.

MARK 3

AZUREAN

AZUREAN
RPCo

Die impressed, 1902 – 1904.

MARK 4

Paper label used on assortment of Rozane shapes with floral and fruit studies that differed slightly from the norm. Hollywood Ware, ca. 1906.

MARK 5

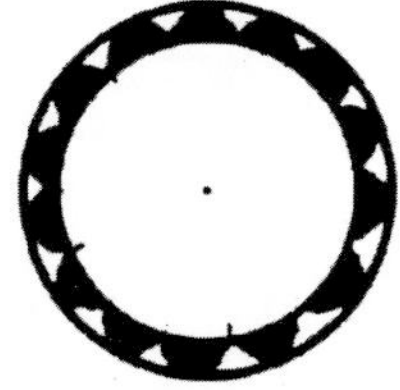

Paper sticker, printed in red ink; applied at the pottery; indicated stock number and retail price.

MARK 6

Applied ceramic seal, late 1904 – early 1906.

Of the many unmarked pieces found today, some were never marked in any way; others originally bore a paper label. If there is evidence of an applied ceramic seal having been removed or mutilated, be advised that the piece in question was a second, sold only through Roseville's outlet, not through the retail market.

Items marked RRPCO, Roseville, Ohio, were made by the Robinson-Ransbottom Pottery Company of Roseville, Ohio. RRPCO is not a Roseville Pottery mark. During the 1970s, Robinson-Ransbottom made a line of jardinieres and pedestals, flowerpots, and vases in a green/brown running glaze reminiscent of items made in the early 1900s. Some were embossed with flowers, others with geometric panels.

MARK 7

Applied ceramic seal with line name in chevron, late 1904 – early 1906.

MARK 8

Fujiyama

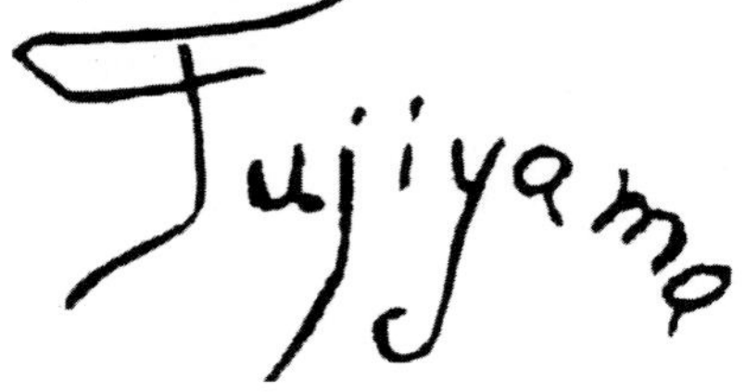

Black ink stamp, 1904.

MARK 9

ROZANE
"OLYMPIC"
POTTERY

Black ink stamp or printed, often includes description of mythological scene, 1905.

MARK 10

Impressed or ink stamp, 1904.

MARK 11

R or R

Usually ink stamped, used until 1928; re-introduced in 1930s for utility ware and Juvenile.

MARK 12

ROSEVILLE
POTTERY CO.
ZANESVILLE, O.

Red ink stamp, ca. 1900 – (?); used on Creamware.

MARK 13

Applied ceramic seal, 1914 – (?)

MARK 14

Impressed, 1915.

MARK 15

ROSEVILLE
ROZANE WARE
POTTERY

Ink stamp, 1917.

MARK 16

Black paper sticker, 1920s – early 1930s.

MARK 17

Silver or gold paper sticker, 1930 – 37.

MARK 18

Roseville
915-5"

Roseville
U.S.A.

Impressed, 1932 – 37.

MARK 19

Be aware that there are many copies of Roseville coming in from China with the Roseville name as shown on the left without the U.S.A. To be authentic, this mark must contain the letters U.S.A.

Roseville
U.S.A.

R U.S.A.

R
U.S.A.

In relief, 1937 – 53.

MARK 20

Lotus

In relief, 1951.

MARK 21

ROSEVILLE
L-23
PASADENA PLANTER
U.S.A.

In relief, 1952.

MARK 22

152L
raymor
by Roseville
U.S.A.
OVENPROOF
PAT. PEND.

In relief, 1952.

Color Album of Pottery

Rozane

Marks: Rozane, RPCo; round Rozane seal; Rozane seal with chevron.

Plate 1*

Vase, 12", #818, (Myers) $500.00–600.00
Vase, 7", #843, artist initialed.......................................$300.00–350.00
Vase, 5", #874, (Myers) $250.00–275.00

* These rare examples of Rozane are highlighted with Aurelian-like orange streaking.

Plate 1

Plate 2

Rozane

Marks: Rozane, RPCo; round Rozane seal; Rozane seal with chevron.

Plate 2

Row 1:

Vase, 9½", (Smith) $3,000.00–4,000.00
Pillow Vase, 8½"...................$2,000.00–2,500.00
Vase, 8½", (Dunlavy)............$2,500.00–3,000.00

Row 2:

Pillow Vase, 9", #882 ....$2,500.00–3,000.00
Vase, 8", (Dunlavy) $2,000.00–2,500.00
Pillow Vase, 9", (Pillsbury)...$2,000.00–2,500.00

Row 3:

Vase, 13", (Leffler) $3,500.00–4,000.00
Vase, 17", #931, (F. Steele) ..$4,000.00–4,500.00
Vase, 14", artist signed.........$3,500.00–4,000.00

Rozane

Marks: Rozane, RPCo; round Rozane seal; Rozane seal with chevron.

Plate 3

Vase, 12", rare sepia-tone glazing, #36, (Pillsbury) $700.00–750.00
Three-sided vase, 8", portraying Morning, Noon, and Night, #1213/188, (EA) $2,000.00–2,500.00
Mug, 5", (Dunlavy) $700.00–800.00

Plate 3

Plate 4

Rozane

Marks: Rozane, RPCo; round Rozane seal; Rozane seal with chevron.

Plate 4

Row 1:

Vase, 5½", #872..................................$150.00–175.00
Vase, 6½", #840/6 ....$125.00–150.00
Vase, 9", (G. Gerwick).........................$150.00–175.00
Vase, 8", (G. Neff)...............................$175.00–200.00
Pillow Vase, 5", #904/7 ....$150.00–175.00

Row 2:

Ewer, 7½", #857/x...............................$175.00–200.00
Vase, 10", (G. Neff).............................$175.00–200.00
Vase, 13", #837/3................................$350.00–400.00
Vase, 11", #902/3 (CLL) $275.00–300.00
Ewer, 7½", #950 ....$175.00–200.00

Row 3:

Vase, 10½", #5....................................$275.00–300.00
Paperweight, 4½", (V. Adams)............$200.00–250.00
Jardiniere, 9½"....................................$175.00–225.00
Vase, 11", #7.......................................$375.00–425.00

Rozane

Marks: Rozane, RPCo; round Rozane Ware seal; Rozane seal with chevron.

Plate 5

3" x 8¼", black lacquered wood faced with a brass plate attached with square brass brads. The metal plate has a black background with a border of two gold lines. "Roseville Pottery" is in red outlined with gold. Made by the American Art Works, Inc., Coshocton, Ohio, who also made Coca-Cola items in the early 1900s. $2,000.00–2,500.00

Plate 5

Plate 6

Rozane

Marks: Rozane, RPCo; round Rozane Ware seal; Rozane seal with chevron.

Plate 6

Row 1:
- Vase, 7¼", (V. Adams)..........................$175.00–200.00
- Tankard, 10½", #821, (CF).................$350.00–400.00
- Candlestick, 9", (J. Imlay) $250.00–275.00
- Vase, 7½", #836 ....$150.00–175.00

Row 2:
- Vase, 8", (Dunlavy)........................$2,500.00–3,000.00
- Pillow Vase, 9", #882, (MT) $2,000.00–2,500.00
- Vase, 7½", (G. Gerwick) $250.00–300.00

Row 3:
- Vase, 14", #891..............................$4,000.00–4,500.00
- Vase, 15", (L. M.)...........................$2,000.00–2,500.00
- Vase, 14", birds and tree blossoms, #891, (W. Myers)....................$3,500.00–4,000.00

A Very Special Offer

(Reprinted from a circa 1900 Roseville ad)

That the delight and value of Rozane, as a true art pottery, may become universally known, we wish to place one piece in your hands, and our booklet in the hands of your friends. We ask you to help us do this. If, therefore, you will have the kindness to send us the full names and correct addresses of ten persons who admire art pottery, or who might become purchasers of Rozane, we will, immediately upon receipt of your list, accompanied by one dollar to cover the cost of packing and shipping, forward you the handsome Envelope Receiver here illustrated. This Receiver is absolutely worth $3.00. It is genuine Rozane Royal, having the same lustrous finish. One of the very prettiest uses to which this holder can be put is to make it a Receiver for letters brought by the postman. It is very handsome upon a desk or hall table, and letters taken from this dainty holder seem all the more welcome, while the appearance of the desk or table is greatly improved by the orderly habit of dropping the mail into this luxurious Receiver.*

* An example of the letter holder described in this ad is pictured below in Row 1.

Rozane

Marks: Rozane, RPCo; round Rozane Ware seals; Rozane seal with chevron.

Plate 7

Row 1:

*Letter Holder, 3½", (C. Neff) $250.00–275.00
Mug, 4½", "Rubba Dub Dub, Three Men in a Tub," stenciled decoration, #856 ... $425.00–450.00
Bud Vase, 6½", #875, (WH) $250.00–275.00
Bud Vase, 6½", #915, artist signed $150.00–175.00
Mug, 5", (G. Gerwick) $150.00–175.00
Mug, 4½", #856, (D) $125.00–150.00

Row 2:

Vase, 10", (M. Timberlake) $650.00–700.00
Vase, 11", (W. Myers) $600.00–650.00
Ewer, 10½", (C. Neff) $300.00–350.00

Row 3:

Vase 13", (Imlay) $425.00–475.00
Tankard, 14", (Imlay) $325.00–375.00
Vase, 18½", #865, (W. Myers) $650.00–750.00
Vase, 15", rare color effect, (V. Adams).. $650.00–700.00
Vase, 10½", rare color effect, (G. Gerwick) $550.00–600.00

Plate 7

Plate 8

Rozane

Marks: Rozane, RPCo; round Rozane Ware seal; Rozane seal with chevron.

Plate 8

Row 1:

Bud Vase, 7½", #841/3, (MN) $150.00–175.00
Bud Vase, 8", (C. Neff) $150.00–175.00
Pillow Vase, 7", (J. Imlay) $275.00–325.00
Vase, 8½", (Timberlake) $175.00–200.00
Vase, 6½", (B. Myers) $150.00–175.00

Row 2:

Vase, 8½" $200.00–225.00
Vase, 10½", (W. Myers) $325.00–375.00

Row 2 (continued):

Pillow Vase, 8½", (V. Adams) $325.00–375.00
Vase, 11", (B. Myers) $250.00–275.00
Vase, 10½" $200.00–225.00

Row 3:

Vase, 14", (H. Pillsbury) $450.00–500.00
Ewer, 16", #858, (W. Myers) $1,250.00–1,500.00
Tankard, 15½", (V. Adams) $1,500.00–2,000.00
Mug, 6", artist signed $250.00–300.00

Plate 9

Rozane

Marks: Rozane, RPCo; round Rozane Ware seal; Rozane seal with chevron.

Plate 9

Row 1:

- Vase, 8", (H.P.) $300.00–350.00
- Vase, 9½", (C. Neff) $225.00–250.00
- Vase, 11½", #833/3 .... $275.00–300.00
- Chocolate Pot, 9½", #936/7, artist signed $500.00–550.00

Row 2:

- Mug, 4", #856/6 .... $150.00–175.00

Row 2 (continued):

- Mug, 6" $225.00–250.00
- Pillow Vase, 7" $250.00–275.00
- Mug, 4", #856/2 .... $175.00–200.00

Row 3:

- Tankard, 16", (J. Imlay) $550.00–600.00
- Vase, 16" $500.00–550.00
- Tankard, 15½", (W. Myers) $450.00–500.00

Plate 10

Plate 11

Vase Assortment #24

Plate 10

- Vase, 8", #107 ....$350.00–400.00
- Vase, 9", #102 ....$275.00–425.00
- Vase, 9", #110 ....$275.00–425.00
- Vase, 8", #108 ....$275.00–425.00
- Vase, 7", #109 ....$325.00–375.00

Azurean

If marked: RPCo, AZUREAN or both.

Plate 11

Row 1:

- Vase, 9"..$2,500.00–3,000.00

Row 2:

- Candlestick, 9", (V. Adams)..............................$900.00–1,000.00
- Vase, 7½", #4, (Leffler)..$575.00–650.00
- Mug, #4 ....$350.00–400.00

Row 3:

- Vase, 14", (W. Myers)...................................$2,500.00–3,000.00
- Vase, 18", #865, (B. Myers)............................$2,000.00–2,500.00
- Vase, 15½", #822/7, (Leffler)..........................$2,000.00–2,500.00

Rozane Light

Marks: Round Rozane seal; Rozane seal with Royal chevron.

Plate 12

HOME ART Jardiniere, 5" $150.00–175.00
Vase, 11½", (W. Myers) $650.00–750.00
Vase, 15", (M. Timberlake)...............$2,500.00–3,000.00

Plate 12

Plate 13

Rozane Light

Marks: Round Rozane seal; Rozane seal with Royal chevron.

Plate 13

Row 1:

Bowl, 3", (MT) $250.00–300.00
Vase, 4", (WM) $200.00–250.00
HOME ART Jardiniere, 5" $150.00–175.00
Mug, 5", (Pillsbury) $300.00–350.00

Row 2:

Pillow Vase, 6½"................................$350.00–400.00
Vase, 8½"", (M. Timberlake) $4,500.00–5,000.00
Pillow Vase, 7", (M. Timberlake)........$400.00–450.00

Row 3:

Vase, 6½", (V. Adams) $300.00–350.00
Vase, 13", (W. Myers)..........................$450.00–500.00
Vase, 18", (MT) $1,250.00–1,500.00
Vase, 14", (MT) $2,500.00–3,000.00
Vase, 8½", (H. Pillsbury)....................$450.00–500.00

Though very similar to Rozane Light in color, the jardinieres shown in Plates 12 and 13 are commonly referred to as Home Art.

The 8½" vase in Plate 13, Row 2, and the 14" vase in Row 3 are both Crystalis shapes decorated with a squeezebag technique similar to Aztec and are quite rare.

Plate 14

Rozane Light

Marks: Round Rozane seal; Rozane seal with Royal chevron.

Plate 14

Row 1:

Sugar Bowl, 4½" $250.00–300.00
Teapot, 8", #60, (Rhead)*................................$6,000.00–7,000.00
Mug, 5", (M. Timberlake).....................................$250.00–300.00

Row 2:

Vase, 8", (J. Imlay)..$350.00–400.00
Vase, 8", (J. Imlay)..$350.00–400.00
Vase, 10", (W. Myers) $450.00–500.00
Vase, 10", (W. Myers) $650.00–750.00
Vase, 8½", (W. Myers) $450.00–550.00

*Done by Frederick Rhead

Row 3:

Tankard, 11", (C. Mitchell) $650.00–700.00
Vase, 11", (H. Pillsbury).......................................$600.00–650.00
Tankard, 16", (L. Mitchell).............................$1,750.00–2,000.00
Vase, 10½", (J. Imlay) $450.00–500.00
Tankard, 10", (J. Imlay), rare corn motif..........$900.00–1,000.00

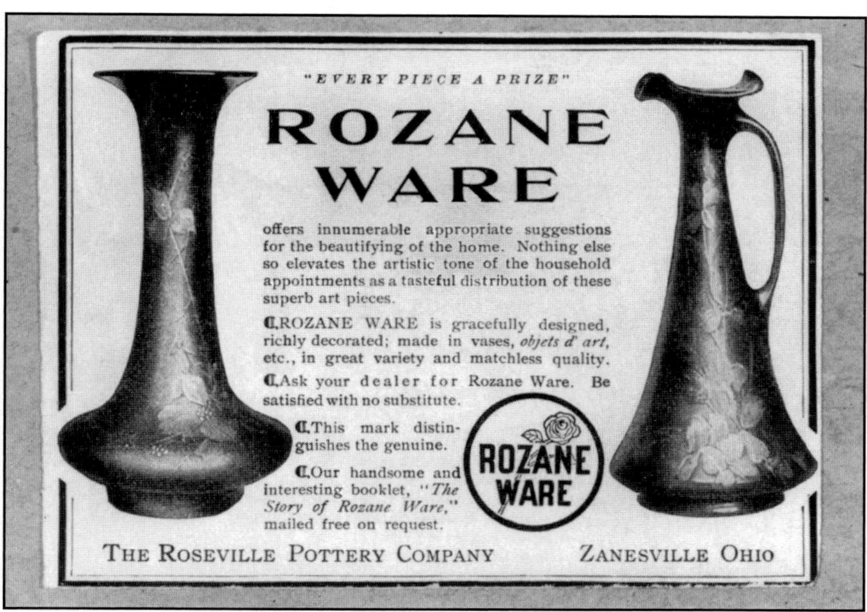

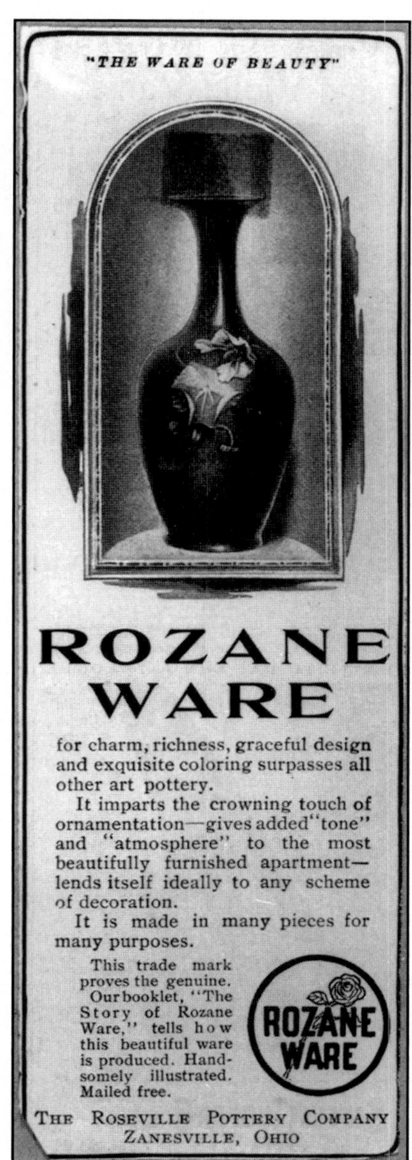

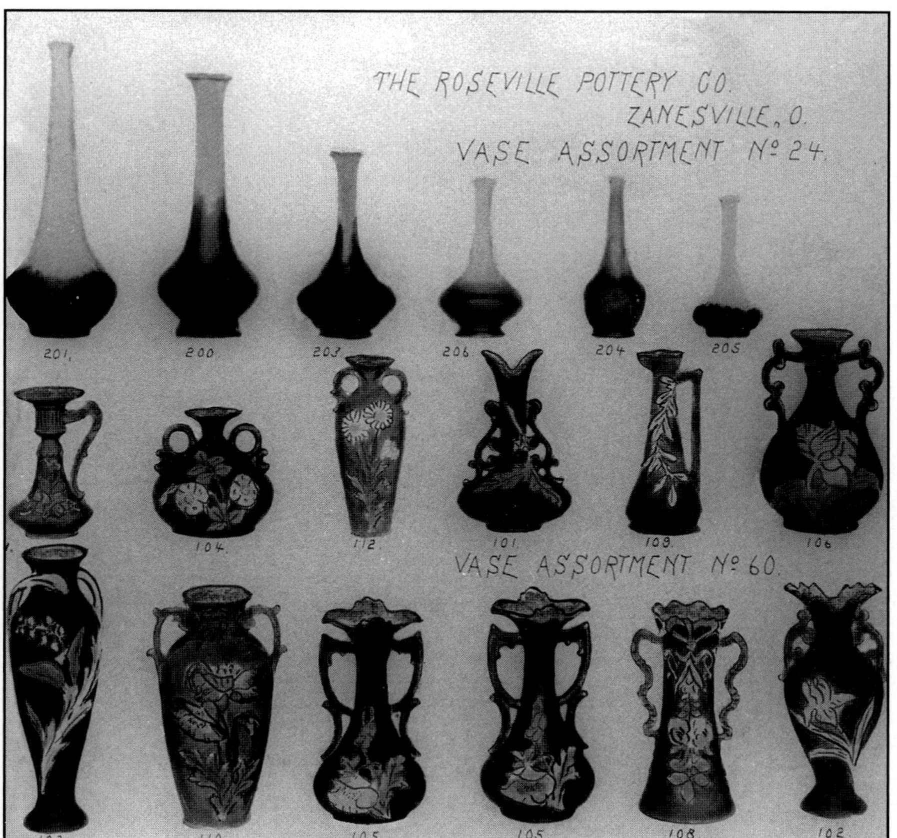

This is the catalog sheet from the Historical Society in Columbus, Ohio, that confirmed the identity of the line of vases shown in Plate 10, page 24.

Plate 15

Plate 16

Mara

If marked: Round Rozane seal; Rozane seal with chevron. Add at least 25% to our values when the Rozane seal is present.

Plate 15
Bowl, 4", (exceptional glaze)............................$2,500.00–3,000.00
Vase, 13", (exceptional glaze)...........................$1,750.00–2,000.00

Plate 16
Vase, 5½", (average glaze)...............................$2,500.00–3,000.00
Vase, 5½", #13, (above average glaze)............$2,000.00–2,500.00

ROZANE MARA...Where the Rainbow Comes From

As changing as the sea, from which it derives its name, and from which, like an opalesque and dainty shell, it seems to have caught every morning hue of iridescence when the sunbeam kissed the spray, Rozane Mara is one of the most decorative as well as one of the most pleasing results yet obtained at the Roseville Potteries.

Studying to obtain the exquisite rainbow tints seen in rarest pieces of old Italian glass, our artist chemist evolved this oddity. The surface, in texture much resembling the lining of the ocean's rarest shells, is somewhat irregular, presenting surfaces most favorable for catching every ray of light, throwing it back in all lustrous shades imaginable. With all this play of colors, Rozane Mara is subdued and in good taste, the prevailing tones running under and through the iridescence being odd reds, varying from pale rose tints to the deepest magentas, the soft tones of gray and opal suggesting the pearly surface of a shell, being always present.

– From an early Rozane Ware catalog

Plate 17

Olympic

Mark: Rozane Olympic Pottery in black ink.

Plate 17

Row 1:

Pitcher, 7", "Ulysses at the Table of Circe" $4,000.00–5,000.00

Pitcher, 7", "Pandora Brought to Earth"........$4,000.00–5,000.00

Row 2:

Vase, 14½", "Persia and Ionia Yoked to the Chariot of Xerxes" $7,500.00–8,500.00

Vase, 20", "Juno Commanding the Sun to Set".......................................$8,000.00–9,000.00

Plate 18

Mongol

If marked: Round Rozane seal; Rozane seal with chevron. Add at least 25% to our values when the Rozane seal is present.

Plate 18

Row 1:

3-Handled Mug, 6", (over-fired) $600.00–700.00

Vase, 5" $450.00–500.00

Row 2:

Vase, 10½", #C-16 ....$3,000.00–3,500.00

Vase, 14" $2,000.00–2,500.00

Vase, 16" $2,000.00–2,500.00

Plate 19

Vase, 8" $900.00–1,000.00

Vase, 10½" $1,100.00–1,250.00

Plate 20

Experimental Vase, 7", (not Mongol, but bears the Mongol seal) $4,000.00–5,000.00

Vase, 2½" $350.00–400.00

From An Early Rozane Ware Catalogue

Rozane Mongol is the name found upon all pieces of Rozane decorated in the rich, beautiful red, known as Sang de Boeuf and which, until very lately, was produced only by the ancient Chinese. For centuries, potters have endeavored to reproduce it, and only in the present generation has this been done. In honor of the famous Mongolian potters who first produced, in pottery, this color of wonderful richness and permanence, the name Mongol was given to this variety of Rozane.

It is a peculiar fact that any one shape reproduced in a number of styles is more admired in this beautiful Mongol red than in any better known color of the day. While ornamentation and design are attractive, especially when viewed by themselves, as single elements of a perfect whole, nothing is better, in the furnishing of a harmonious room, than art objects in a simple color, wisely placed to lend just the right, pleasing effect to the eye.

A late writer, comparing vases of plain color and those decorated, gives a vivid figure by comparing those of one color to the single musical notes which, combined, produce a harmony. Were each a complete tune, simultaneously sounded, the result would be a jangling discord.

Thus, while elaborate decoration is desirable for certain places (against a plain wall, a drapery of plain material or in a niche by itself), as a unit in the decoration of an entire room, the vase of single color, or in varying hues of the same color, is often most pleasing — most harmonious.

To this harmony is added still another result upon a room by the addition of a piece of Rozane Mongol — its effect of richness.

It is the famous, long-sought red of the Chinese revealing many harmonious hues made brilliant by any reflections, in its glaze, from window or artificial light, and wherever placed the Mongol vase imparts a rich, luxurious touch of warmth, needed in every room where a feeling of comfort is desired.

Plate 19

Plate 20

Plate 21

BLUE WARE Vase, 6", This vase contained this note of verification: Bought from daughter of J. F. Weaver, Vice-president of first Rv officers. This vase made by Roseville Pottery and designed by Fujiyama. (signed) Evan Purviance $1,500.00–2,000.00

BLUE WARE Pitcher, 7½" $3,500.00–4,500.00

WOODLAND Vase, 11" $8,000.00–9,000.00

Plate 21

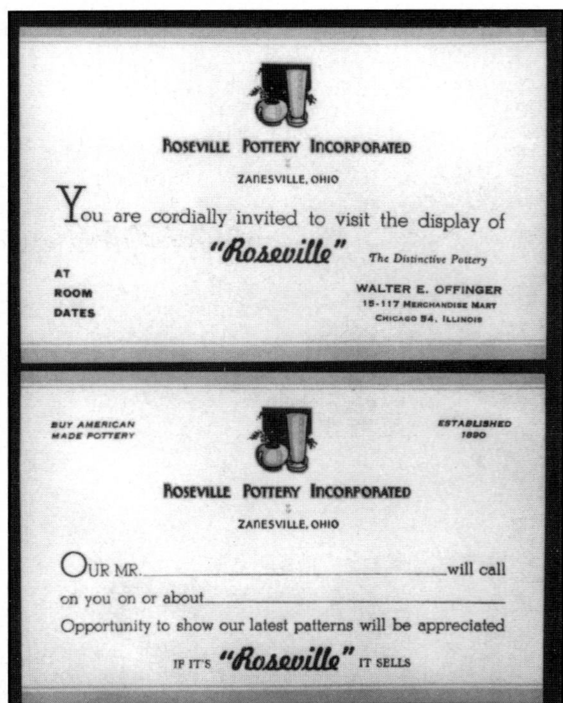

ROSEVILLE POTTERY INCORPORATED

ZANESVILLE, OHIO

You are cordially invited to visit the display of

"Roseville" The Distinctive Pottery

AT

ROOM

DATES

WALTER E. OFFINGER

15-117 MERCHANDISE MART

CHICAGO 54, ILLINOIS

BUY AMERICAN MADE POTTERY

ESTABLISHED 1890

ROSEVILLE POTTERY INCORPORATED

ZANESVILLE, OHIO

OUR MR.________________will call

on you on or about________________

Opportunity to show our latest patterns will be appreciated

IF IT'S "Roseville" IT SELLS

Paper collectibles such as these display invitations are always of interest to collectors. $25.00 – 35.00.

From An Early Rozane Ware Catalog

ROZANE WOODLAND...Ancient Spirit of Modern Art. We do not deny that the resemblance of Rozane Woodland to one of the oldest and rarest of Chinese potteries is no accident. While Woodland is not an attempt at imitation of the old Chinese Celadon, familiarity with the latter, and with its exquisite qualities, was inspiration to the artist who created the idea of Rozane Woodland. Old Celadon, like Woodland, was decorated by incising either floral or conventional designs in the moist clay, or biscuit, after moulding, and was further ornamented by studs or dots. The old Celadon was very hard, opaque, closely akin to stoneware, and covered with a partially translucent enamel. There were vases of gray earth shading into browns and yellows and scattered with little laminae of mica, or sometimes picked with tiny points, almost imperceptible. The value of old pieces in this style is almost inestimable.

The description of Rozane Woodland is almost identical with this of the old Chinese ware, except that Woodland has not the mica. The laminae mentioned, however, are daintily picked into the surface of the softly shaded mat background, lending just an agreeable relief from its plainness, which is further broken by the dots or "studs," while the enameled designs stand out in pleasant contrast. The latter are usually in foliage hues, the browns resembling late autumn woodlands, when the dun, frost-exposed oak leaves — brown, mellow and glossy — still cling, rustling, in final glory, to the trees.

Rozane Woodland is exceptionally beautiful in every point that contributes to the excellence of an art pottery. It is a pleasure to present this as our final argument for the true worth of Rozane.

Plate 22

Woodland

If marked: Round Rozane seal; Rozane seal with chevron. Add at least 25% to our values when the Rozane seal is present.

Plate 22

Row 1:

- Vase, 6" $450.00–500.00
- Vase, 6½" $600.00–650.00
- Vase, 6½" $500.00–550.00
- Vase, 7" $500.00–550.00

Row 2:

- Vase, 9" $800.00–900.00
- Vase, 9" $650.00–700.00
- Vase, 11" $750.00–800.00
- Vase, 11½" $750.00–800.00

Row 2 (continued):

- Vase, 10" $850.00–900.00
- Vase, 9" $700.00–750.00

Row 3:

- Vase, 13" $4,000.00–4,500.00
- Vase, 19" $6,000.00–7,000.00
- Vase, 15½", (ET) $2,000.00–2,500.00
- Vase, 15" $2,500.00–3,000.00

Paper collectibles such as these stationery items are always of interest to collectors. $25.00 – 35.00.

Fudji

If marked: Round Rozane seal; Rozane seal with chevron. Add at least 25% to our values when this Rozane seal is present.

Plate 23

- Vase, 9"..$2,500.00–3,000.00
- Vase, 10½"..................................$4,000.00–4,500.00
- Vase, 10", (E)...............................$3,500.00–4,000.00

Plate 23

Plate 24

Fujiyama

Mark: Fujiyama ink stamp.

Plate 24

- Vase, 15"....................................$2,750.00–3,000.00
- Jardiniere, 9".............................$3,500.00–4,000.00
- Vase, 11"....................................$2,500.00–2,750.00
- Vase, 9"......................................$2,500.00–2,750.00

Paper label found on first Mug in Row 2: below.

Della Robbia

If marked: Round Rozane seal.

Plate 25

Row 1:

- Teapot, 6", (EB) $2,000.00–2,500.00
- Teapot, 5½", Inscription: If a woman says she will, she will, depend on it. But if she says she won't, she won't and there's an end on't, (KD and ER) $2,000.00–2,500.00
- Teapot, 6" $2,250.00–2,750.00

Row 2:

- Mug, 4½", (HS) $900.00–1,000.00
- Pitcher, 8", (KE) $3,500.00–4,000.00
- Mug, 4½", (FB) $600.00–700.00

Plate 25

Plate 26

Della Robbia

If marked: Round Rozane seal.

Plate 26

Row 1:

- Tankard, 10½", (HS) $4,500.00–5,000.00
- Teapot, 6½" $2,500.00–3,000.00
- Tankard, 10½". Inscription: A Chirping Cup is my Matin Song. And the Vesper Bell is My Bowl. Ding Dong!, (MF) $2,000.00–2,500.00

Row 2:

- Vase, 10", (MH) $7,000.00–8,000.00
- Vase, 11", (GC)? $2,500.00–3,000.00
- Vase, 9", (H. Smith) $2,000.00–2,500.00

Della Robbia

If marked: Round Rozane seal.

Plate 27

Row 1:

- Vase, 8", (GB)....$8,000.00–9,000.00
- Teapot, 8", (K)....$2,000.00–2,500.00
- Vase, 8½", (ME)....$5,000.00–6,000.00

Row 2:

- Mug, 4", (KD)....$600.00–700.00
- Jar, 8",
  - (shown without lid), (-G-)....$4,500.00–5,500.00
  - (with lid)....$8,000.00–9,000.00
- Vase, 9½", (EC)....$4,000.00–4,500.00
- Bowl, 8" x 2½", (HS)....$5,000.00–5,500.00
- Letter Holder, 3½"....$1,250.00–1,500.00

Row 3:

- Vase, 15", (–Golde–)....$9,000.00–10,000.00
- Vase, 14", (H. Smith)....$10,000.00–12,500.00
- Vase, 11½", (FB)....$25,000.00–30,000.00
- Vase, 11½", (HL)....$15,000.00–17,500.00

Plate 28

- Vase, 19", (HL)....$30,000.00–35,000.00

Plate 29

- Vase, 12", (EC)....$20,000.00–25,000.00

Plate 30

- Vase, 8½", (H. Smith)....$4,500.00–5,000.00

Plate 27

Plate 28

Plate 29

Plate 30

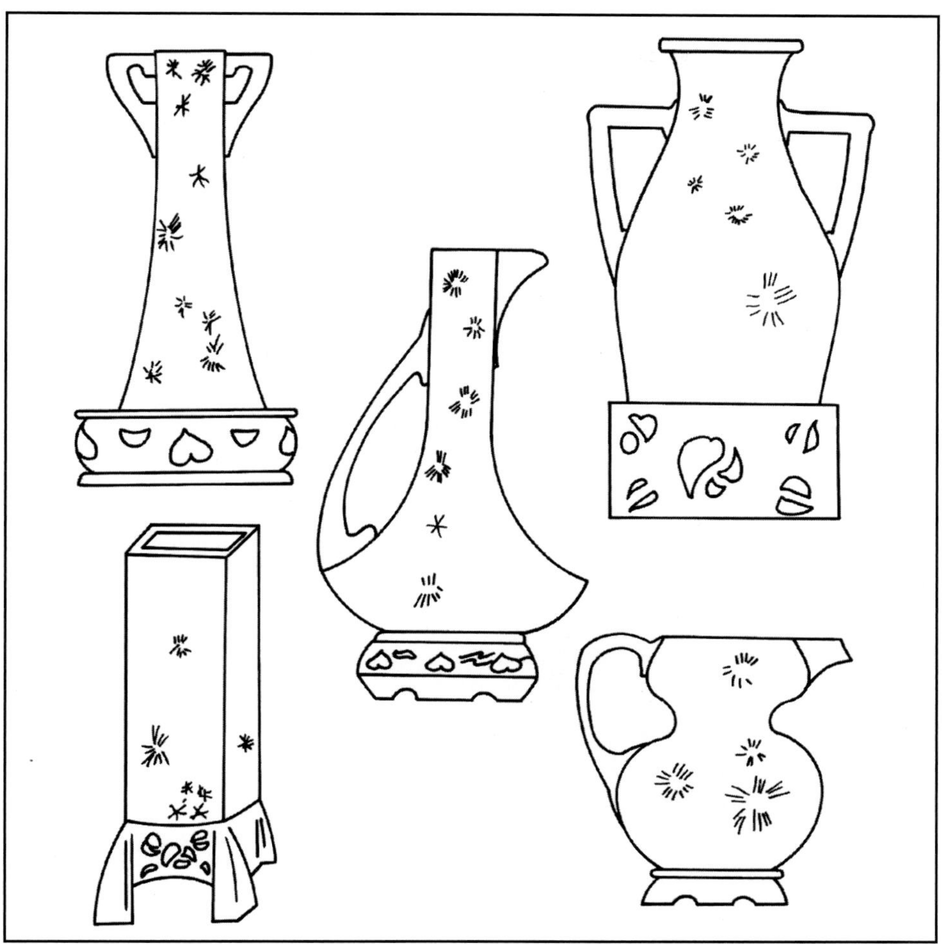

These line drawings are representative of some proposed Crystalis shapes found in the original Roseville files.

Crystalis

If marked: Round Rozane seal.

Plate 31

Vase, 14"................................$4,000.00–5,000.00
Pot, 3"....................................$1,750.00–2,000.00

In addition to the round Rozane seal, Crystalis shapes are often found with a Mongol chevron for this reason: Many blanks were pre-produced with Mongol seals in anticipation of full-scale marketing, but when it became apparent that the Mongol glaze was too difficult to achieve on a consistent basis, the line was discontinued. Rather than discard the unused blanks, Roseville utilized the often thick and gloppy Crystalis glaze, allowing it to run down into the seal and, in most cases, obliterating it completely.

Plate 31

Plate 32

Crystalis

If marked: Round Rozane seal. Add at least 25% to our values when the Rozane seal is present.

Plate 32

- Candlestick, 9" $1,000.00–1,250.00
- Vase, 12½" $4,000.00–4,500.00
- Vase, 13" $2,000.00–2,500.00
- Vase, 11" $3,000.00–3,500.00
- Vase, 5½" $1,250.00–1,500.00

Various Early Lines

If marked: Round Rozane seal.

Plate 33

Row 1:

- Vase, 3½", (H. Rhead) $900.00–1,000.00
- WATER LILY Planter/Liner, 4", squeezebag decoration $400.00–500.00
- GOLD Vase, 7", #501 ....$400.00–500.00
- MARA Vase, 5½", (overfired) $600.00–700.00

Row 2:

- Vase, 11", sgraffito decoration $1,500.00–1,750.00
- DECORATED LANDSCAPE Vase, 9", sgraffito and squeezebag, artist signed $2,500.00–3,000.00
- Vase, 8½", stencil technique $900.00–1,000.00
- Vase, determined recently to be Weller Pottery.
- Vase, 12", transfer with gold, sometimes referred to as Gibson Girl $2,000.00–2,500.00

Plate 33

Plate 34

Blue Ware

Plate 34

Mug, 6" $450.00–500.00
Teapot, 8" $450.00–500.00
Teapot, 7" $800.00–900.00
Teapot, 4" $350.00–400.00

Special

If marked: RPCo.

Plate 35

Mug, 5" $200.00–250.00
Tankard, 12" $400.00–450.00
Mug, 5" $175.00–225.00
Tankard, 15½", #884 ....$550.00–600.00

Specials as indicated in the Roseville catalog were decorated with transfers over a highly refined body closely resembling fine painted china. Early Rozane shapes were often used, which determines this ware to be from the early 1900s.

Plate 35

Plate 36

Plate 36

Pillow Vase, hand-painted
cupid portrait, 9", #882...................$8,000.00–9,000.00
SPECIAL vase, 9" $350.00–450.00

Decorated Art

If marked: As illustrated below.

Plate 37
Row 1:

Jardiniere, 8" $300.00–350.00
Vase, 12½", #20 .... $1,250.00–1,500.00
Jardiniere, 6" $175.00–225.00

Decorated Art is a rather broad term adopted by collectors to refer to the less detailed, often Art Nouveau style of decoration as shown in Plate 37. Often gold tracing is used for a lovely accent. The molds for these are also early 1900.

Row 2:

Jardiniere, 10", #448 .... $500.00–600.00
The unusual mark pictured below also appeared on this item.
Vase, 16" $1,500.00–1,750.00

Plate 37

These green glazes (below and on pages 41 and 42) sometimes vary from a very dark tone to an unusually light color. Some pieces have a rubbery appearance or are peppered with dark speckles. Egypto evolved from the earlier Chloron and in later years became simply Matt Green. Remember that only pieces with the Egypto wafer can accurately be identified as Egypto. The appearance of their bases can help distinguish Chloron (which has a buff-colored base, either matt or glossy) from Matt Green (whose color extends completely over the outside surface, wrapping around sides and across bottom with no interruption.

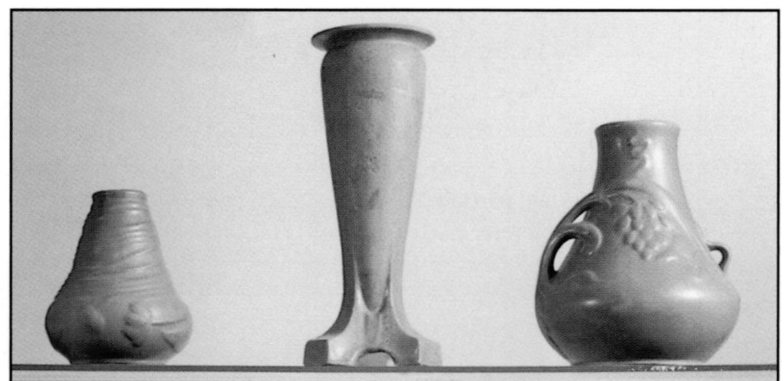

Plate 38

Chloron

If marked: Chloron impressed or ink stamp; TRPCo (mark illustrated above).

Plate 38
Row 1:

Vase, 6½" $450.00–500.00
Vase, 12" $900.00–1,000.00
Vase, 9" $800.00–900.00

From An Early Rozane Ware Catalog

ROZANE EGYPTO...Thought Made Permanent in Pottery. Rozane Egypto may be classed as one of the oddest styles of Rozane, although its soft finish and coloring, in varying shades of old greens, suggest a very beautiful color found in some of the rarest and most ancient potteries of old Egypt. The shapes and decorations, too, are reproductions of Egyptian art antiques. Each piece of Rozane Egypto expresses a complete thought of its artist, savoring of the restfulness and freedom of nature. Through the shades of old green are seen glintings of those rich violets and blues which often entered into the colorings of rarest old Egyptian pieces. The prevailing color of these latter was a green which came to be almost as famous as the old red of the Chinese.

— Rozane Egypto is indispensable in a collection of Rozanes — or of any pottery. Not only is the color itself peculiarly attractive and restful, but the forms in this variety, like all Rozanes, are graceful and well proportioned. The low modelings of matt decoration retaining the prevailing hues, contribute effectively to its beauty.

Plate 39

Egypto

Mark: Round Rozane seal. All Egypto must have this seal.

Plate 39

- Pitcher Vase, 11" $1,500.00–1,750.00
- Lamp Base/Urn, 10"....................$3,500.00–4,500.00
- Vase, 6½" $600.00–700.00
- Pitcher, 7"..$600.00–700.00
- Vase, 5½" $550.00–600.00

Matt Green

Mark: None.

Plate 40

Row 1:

- Pot/Liner, 3" $75.00–100.00
- Pot/Liner, 3" $100.00–125.00
- Pot/Liner, 4" $100.00–125.00
- Gate, 5" x 8" $100.00–125.00
- Pot/Frog, 2½" $100.00–125.00

Row 2:

- Jardiniere, 6"....................................$250.00–300.00
- Tobacco Jar, 6".................................$300.00–350.00
- Planter/Liner, 4" x 8"........................$450.00–500.00
- Jardiniere, 5½", #456 .... $250.00–300.00

Plate 40

Plate 41

Chloron, Egypto, and Matt Green

Plate 41
Top:
MATT GREEN, Hanging Basket, 9"......................$175.00–200.00
Row 1:
MATT GREEN, Scarab Planter/Liner, 4", #510...$250.00–300.00
CHLORON, Candlestick, 4" $250.00–300.00
EGYPTO, Creamer, 3½" $350.00–400.00
EGYPTO, Bud Vase, 5½"......................................$400.00–450.00
CHLORON, Bowl, 3" $250.00–300.00

Row 2:
CHLORON, Jardiniere, 5½", #487........................$400.00–450.00
CHLORON, Vase, 7" $850.00–950.00
CHLORON, Vase, 9" $900.00–1,000.00
Row 3:
EGYPTO, Vase, 12½" $1,500.00–1,750.00
EGYPTO, Pitcher, 12".....................................$1,250.00–1,500.00
EGYPTO, Circle Jug, 11", rare........................$4,000.00–5,000.00
MATT GREEN, Planter, original brass housing, 5½" $300.00–350.00

Pauleo

If marked: Pauleo ceramic seal; paper sticker as illustrated on page 44.

Plate 42

Vase, 19", #340...$1,500.00–2,000.00
Bowl, 3", ...$800.00–900.00
Vase, 19", ...$2,500.00–3,000.00

Plate 42

Plate 43

Pauleo

If marked: Pauleo seal; paper sticker as illustrated on page 44.

Plate 43
Row 1:

Vase, 9"...$700.00–800.00
Vase, 12", paper label........................$1,500.00–1,750.00
Vase, 9"...$700.00–800.00

Row 2:

Vase, 18½"* $3,000.00–3,500.00
Vase, 19"...$1,500.00–2,000.00
Vase, 20½" $2,000.00–2,500.00

* This vase is marked with the very rare ceramic seal.

Pauleo – From a booklet titled "Pauleo Pottery" presented by the Roseville Company in 1916 comes the information that up until that time, at least, Pauleo was never decorated. The company emphasized this point elaborately, stating that its aesthetic value was accented by its simplicity — a "leaving off of adornment." But its unusual, varied glazes stirred enough excitement to make it a very popular seller. A Roseville Pottery shop, whose primary purpose was to sell Pauleo creations, was opened in New York on 50th Street and 5th Avenue. George Young, Harry Rhead, and C.E. Offinger themselves took charge of Pauleo production. Only during the next few years was decoration added to the Pauleo line. Finally thick matt glazes were introduced, later the catalyst for Carnelian II.

Plate 44

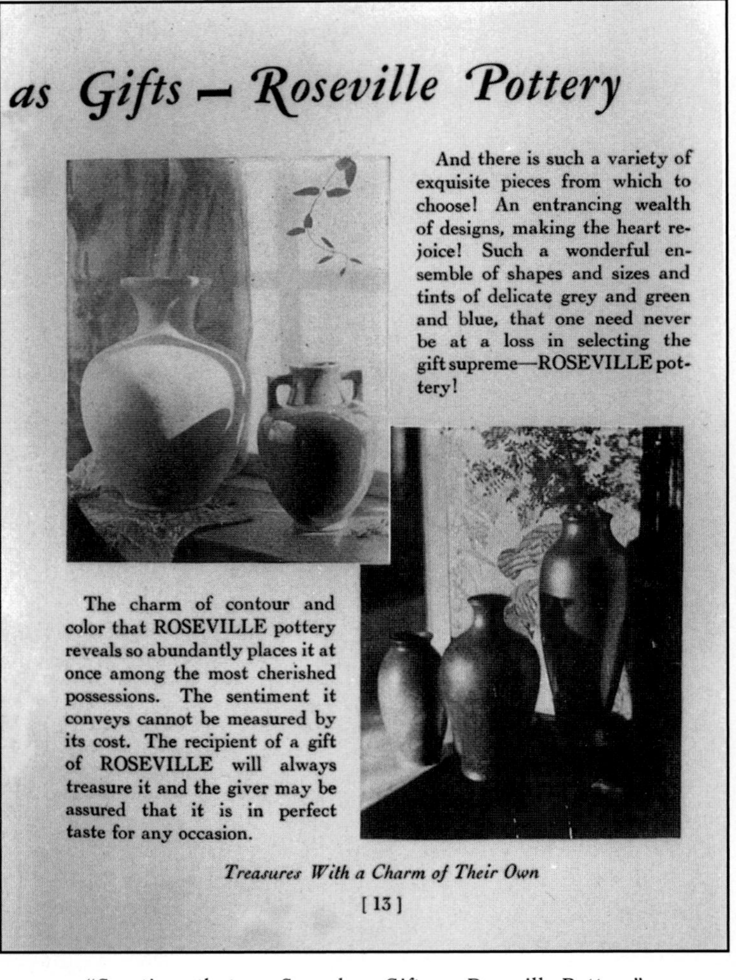

as Gifts – Roseville Pottery

And there is such a variety of exquisite pieces from which to choose! An entrancing wealth of designs, making the heart rejoice! Such a wonderful ensemble of shapes and sizes and tints of delicate grey and green and blue, that one need never be at a loss in selecting the gift supreme—ROSEVILLE pottery!

The charm of contour and color that ROSEVILLE pottery reveals so abundantly places it at once among the most cherished possessions. The sentiment it conveys cannot be measured by its cost. The recipient of a gift of ROSEVILLE will always treasure it and the giver may be assured that it is in perfect taste for any occasion.

Treasures With a Charm of Their Own

[13]

"Creations that are Superb as Gifts — Roseville Pottery"
Company Booklet

Old company photo illustrating Pauleo shape.

Pauleo

If marked: Pauleo seal; paper sticker illustrated on page 44.

Plate 45
Row 1:
Vase, 17" $1,500.00–2,000.00
Vase, 14" $1,500.00–2,000.00
Row 2:
Vase, 17½" $1,250.00–1,500.00
Vase, 19" $1,500.00–2,000.00
Vase, 16½" $1,250.00–1,500.00

Plate 45

Plate 46

Pauleo

If marked: Pauleo seal; paper sticker illustrated on page 44.

Plate 46

Row 1:

Vase, 16½"* $2,500.00–3,000.00
Vase, 14" $1,500.00–1,750.00
Vase, 16½" $1,250.00–1,500.00

* This vase is marked with the very rare ceramic seal.

Row 2:

Vase, 15½" $4,500.00–5,500.00
Vase, 17" $3,500.00–4,000.00

This Holland stein set was a promotional item offered by a beer company.

Cornelian, Colonial, Venetian, and Holland

Mark: None.

Plate 47

Row 1:

- CORNELIAN Shaving Mug, 4"....................$65.00–75.00
- CORNELIAN Mush Bowl, 3" & Pitcher, 5½"....................$80.00–100.00
- CORNELIAN Toothbrush Holder, 5"..........$60.00–70.00
- CORNELIAN Soap Dish, 4"........................$75.00–85.00

Row 2:

- COLONIAL Soap Dish, 4"..........................$80.00–90.00
- VENETIAN Salesman's Sample, marked Venetian, #3 (?).....................$70.00–80.00
- CORNELIAN Shaving Mug, 4"....................$65.00–75.00
- HOLLAND Pitcher, 12"..........................$400.00–500.00

Row 3:

- CORNELIAN Pitcher, 12" & Bowl, 15½"...$350.00–450.00
- COLONIAL, Combinet, 12"....................$300.00–350.00

Plate 47

Cornelian

Mark: None.

Plate 48

Row 1:

Pitcher, 4"................................$50.00–60.00
Pitcher, 5"................................$75.00–85.00
"Wild Rose" Pitcher, 9".......$125.00–150.00
Pitcher with Wheat, 5½"........$75.00–85.00
Pitcher with Corn, 5"..........$125.00–150.00

Row 2:

"Corn" Pitcher, 6"...............$125.00–150.00
"Our Leader" Jardiniere, 7"..$95.00–110.00
"Our Leader" Jardiniere, 6½", #119...................$100.00–125.00

Plate 48

Plate 49

Colonial

Mark: None.

Plate 49

Pitcher, 7½"........................$100.00–125.00
Pitcher, 11".........................$175.00–250.00
Bowl, 16"............................$150.00–200.00
Toothbrush Holder, 5"............$85.00–95.00

Holland

Mark: None.

Plate 50

Powder Jar, 3".........................$125.00–150.00
Tankard, #2, 9½"....................$200.00–250.00
Pitcher, #1, 6½"......................$200.00–250.00
Mug, 4".......................................$60.00–75.00

Plate 50

Plate 51

Plate 52

Aztec

If marked: None.

Plate 51

Vase, 9", (E)....................$400.00–500.00
Vase, 11", (R)....................$800.00–900.00
Vase, 11"....................$600.00–700.00
Vase, 9"....................$400.00–500.00
Vase, 8", (R)....................$400.00–500.00

Plate 52

Vase, 11½"....................$500.00–600.00
Vase, 10½"....................$400.00–500.00
Vase, 9½"....................$400.00–500.00

Shiny Aztec or Crocus...whatever the term you choose to refer to this ware (we find nothing official), consider it synonymous with "rare," "beautiful," and certainly "desirable" for your collection. Although a few shapes from this line are also used in the Aztec line, the same shapes were also used in Della Robbia as well as some Rozane lines. Some shapes, Plate 53, #1 and Plate 54, #2, seem exclusive to this line. The decoration is slip work, rather than squeezebag.

Plate 53

Plate 54

Crocus

If marked: Rozane Ware seal.

Plate 53

Vase, 7" $650.00–750.00
Vase, 9½", (CB) $750.00–850.00
Vase, 9" $750.00–850.00
Vase, 7" $650.00–750.00

Plate 54

Vase, 9", (GS) $750.00–850.00
Vase, 7" $500.00–550.00
Vase, 6", Rozane Ware seal, (PD) $650.00–750.00
Letter Receiver, 3½" $400.00–450.00

Plate 55

Early Pitchers
Mark: None.

Plate 55

Row 1:

OSIRIS Utility Pitcher, 6½"..................................$100.00–125.00

OSIRIS Pitcher, 8"..$125.00–150.00

Row 2:

"The Grape" Pitcher, 6", "Compliments of Magee Furnace Co." (This particular pitcher was a promotional item.)..$175.00–225.00

Row 2 (continued):

"The Boy" Pitcher, 7½"...$400.00–500.00

"The Grape" Pitcher, 6"..$150.00–175.00

Row 3:

"Goldenrod" Pitcher, 9½"....................................$250.00–300.00

"The Mill" Pitcher, 8"...$450.00–500.00

"Wild Rose" Pitcher, 9½"......................................$200.00–250.00

Early Pitchers

Mark: None.

Plate 56

"Poppy" Pitcher, 9", #11 ....$350.00–400.00
"Poppy" Pitcher, 9", #141 ....$300.00–350.00

Plate 56

Plate 57

Early Pitchers

Mark: None.

Plate 57

Row 1:
"The Bridge" Pitcher, 6" $150.00–175.00
"Iris" Pitcher, 7" $400.00–450.00
Blended "Bridge" Pitcher, 6" $100.00–125.00

Row 2:
"Landscape" Pitcher, 7½" $150.00–175.00
Undecorated "Tulip" Pitcher, R #18, U.S.A., 1930s reissue ..$100.00–125.00
"Tulip" Pitcher, 7½" $150.00–175.00

Row 3:
"The Cow" Pitcher, 7½" $350.00–400.00
"The Cow" Pitcher, 6½", (rare size) $400.00–450.00
"The Cow" Pitcher, 7½" $400.00–450.00

Plate 58

Blended Glaze & Early Pitchers

Mark: None.

Plate 58

Row 1:
- Vase, 7" $75.00–100.00
- BLENDED Tankard, 12", #890 .... $150.00–200.00
- BLENDED Vase, 6½" $75.00–100.00

Row 2:
- GERMAN COOKING WARE Pitcher, 3" $60.00–70.00
- BLENDED Vase, 3" $75.00–85.00
- BLENDED Vase, 5½" $85.00–95.00
- BLENDED Vase, 4", #817 .... $95.00–110.00

Row 3:
- "The Owl" Pitcher, 6½" $550.00–600.00
- BLENDED Pitcher, 7" $100.00–125.00
- BLENDED "Grape" Pitcher, 6" $100.00–125.00

Row 4:
- BLENDED "Landscape" Pitcher, 7½" $125.00–150.00
- "Wild Rose" with gold tracing, 9" $150.00–175.00
- BLENDED "Holland," 9½" $150.00–200.00
- ROZANE Pitcher, 8½", #886, (W. Myers) $400.00–500.00

Plate 59

Canvassers Outfit, before 1898

Plate 59
- Red Apple Bank, 2¾" x 3½" $350.00–400.00
- Yellow Apple Bank, 3" x 4" $350.00–400.00
- Orange Bank, 3¼" x 3½" $350.00–400.00

The old ad below identified these banks as Roseville Pottery, and their Roseville, Ohio, address dates their production before 1898 when the main office was moved to Zanesville.

CANVASSERS OUTFIT — Entire outfit, $1.00 ppd. Included: #90 min. umbrella stand, 3" x 7"...50¢ (#91 was shown, the same as #90, different motif); #228 min. cuspidor, 3" wide...20¢ (#219, #221, and #201 were the same cuspidor, different decoration); #315 min. cooking crock...10¢ (ad says "too well known to need comment"); #221 apple bank and #120 orange bank...10¢ each, finished to represent fruit. ANY CANVASSER WITH THIS OUTFIT CAN MAKE $4 to $6 PER DAY.

Banks and novelties were produced at the turn of the century in many colors...green, blue, blended, spongeware, and dark brown. Some were hand decorated. By observation, one collector has been able to determine the identity of some of these early unmarked, uncatalogued novelties — the monkey figural bottles and "Ye Old Time" jugs. All are known to exist in the five glaze colors, as well as hand decorated; all had identical bases and were made of the very light colored clay.

Banks

Marks: None.

Plate 60

Row 1:
- Jug, 4", "Ye Olden Time" $100.00–125.00
- Monkey Bottle, 5½" $100.00–125.00
- *Monkey Bottle, 6", rare glaze $450.00–500.00
- Monkey Bottle, 5½" $100.00–125.00

Row 2:
- Eagle, 2½" $400.00–450.00
- Lion, 2½" $450.00–500.00
- Cat, 4" $450.00–500.00
- Beehive, 3" $450.00–500.00
- Beehive, 2½" $400.00–450.00

*Also made as a bank, very rare, $600.00 – 700.00

Plate 61

Row 1:
- Pig, 2½" x 5" $175.00–200.00
- Large Pig, 4" x 5½" $350.00–400.00
- Pig, 3" x 4", "St. Louis, 1904," commemorative $225.00–250.00

Row 2:
- Buffalo, 3" x 6" $350.00–400.00
- Dog, 4" $450.00–500.00
- Uncle Sam, 4" $200.00–225.00
- Buffalo, 3" x 6½" $350.00–400.00

Plate 60

Plate 61

Plate 62

Cremo

Mark: None.

Plate 62

Vase, 7" $3,500.00–4,000.00

Autumn

Mark: None.

Plate 63

Row 1:

Pitcher, 8½" $400.00–450.00

Toothbrush Holder, 5" $275.00–325.00

Shaving Mug, 4".....................$275.00–325.00

Soap Dish/Liner, 5½" across.......................$300.00–350.00

Row 2:

Wash Bowl, 14½"....................$300.00–350.00

Pitcher, 12½"..........................$450.00–500.00

Set $850.00–1,000.00

Jardiniere, 9½".......................$600.00–700.00

Plate 63

Sylvan
Mark: None.

Plate 64
Vase, 9½" $600.00–700.00
Jardiniere, 9" $600.00–700.00

Plate 64

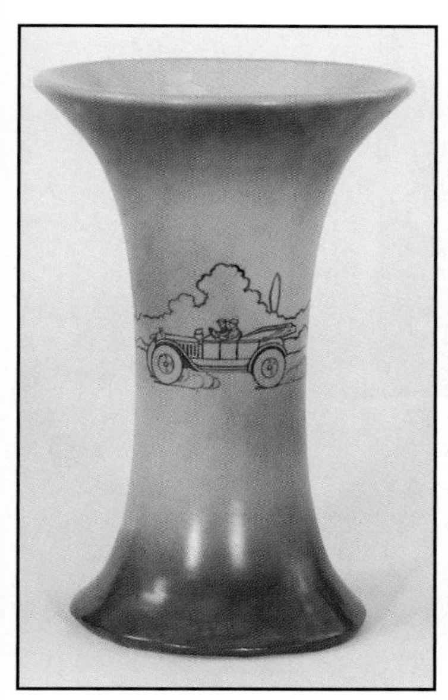

Plate 65

Plate 66

Tourist Variation
Mark: None.

Plate 65
Unusual Vase, 9" $500.00–600.00
Creamware with olive green shading, black scene.

Tourist
Mark: None.

Plate 66
Window Box, 8½" x 19" $5,000.00–6,000.00
Vase, 8" $1,500.00–2,000.00

Plate 67

Novelty Steins

Mark: None.

Plate 67

Row 1:
- 5", "Try it on the dog..." $250.00–300.00
- 4½", "It's an ill will wind that blows nobody good" $250.00–300.00
- 5", "There must be some mistake" $250.00–300.00

Row 2:
- 4½", "Butting in" $250.00–300.00
- 5", "Do it now" $250.00–300.00
- 5", "Better late than never" $250.00–300.00

Row 3:
- 5", "Made in Germany" $250.00–300.00

Row 3 (continued):
- 4½", "It's up to you" $250.00–300.00
- 5", "Ain't it hell to be poor," Compliments of E. Hilfreich, 25 Flushing Ave., Astoria, L.I., N.Y $250.00–300.00

Row 4:
- 4½", "No vacation in this business" $250.00–300.00
- 4½", "This is so sudden" $250.00–300.00
- 4½", "Protection for infant industry" $250.00–300.00

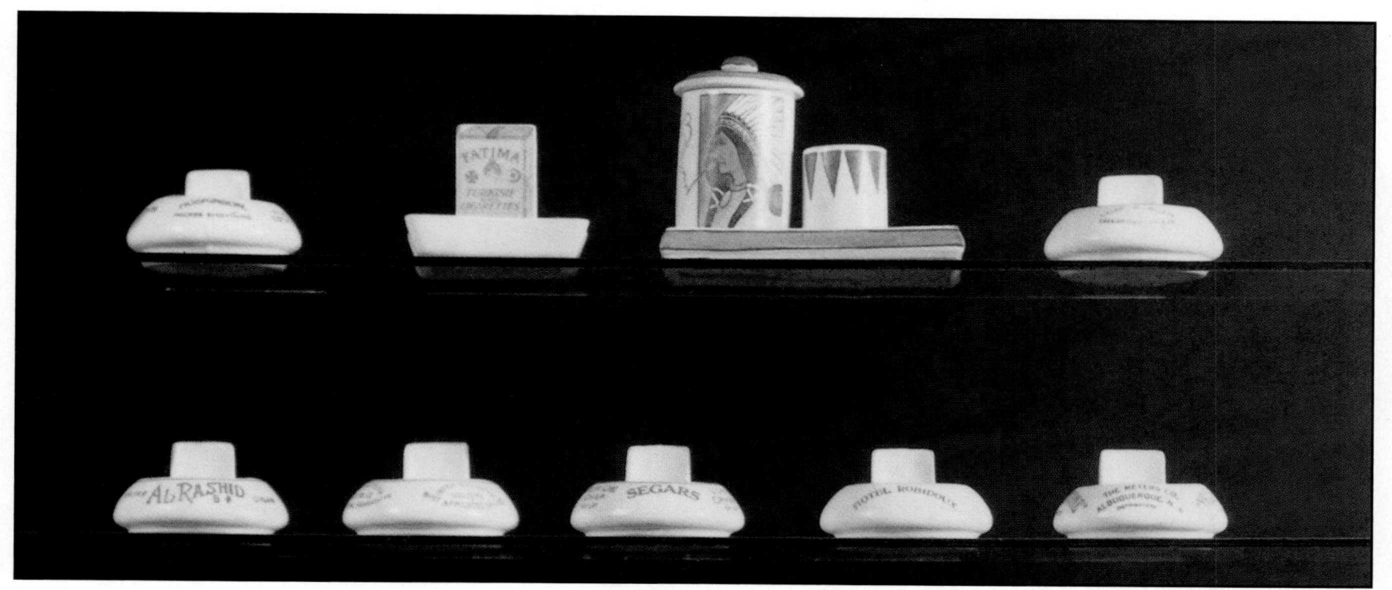

Plate 68

Plate 69

Smoker Sets

Mark: Generally none.

Plate 68

Row 1:

Ashtray, 2", Roseville Pottery Co., Zanesville, Ohio, red ink stamp $60.00–75.00

Ashtray "Fatima," 3" $250.00–300.00

Indian Smoker Set, 4½" x 6½" $550.00–600.00

Ashtray, 2" $60.00–75.00

Row 2:

Ashtrays, 2" $60.00–75.00

Plate 69

Tobacco Jar, 6" $250.00–300.00

Combination set with Indian, 7½" $650.00–700.00

Combination "Bachelor's Coat of Arms," 7½" $275.00–350.00

Jar, 4½" $125.00–150.00

Plate 70

Donatella Tea Sets

Mark: None.

Plate 70

Row 1:
FORGET-ME-NOT; Creamer, 3"; Pot, 6½"; Sugar, 3½"
- Set $300.00–350.00
- Creamer $60.00–70.00
- Sugar with Lid $70.00–80.00

Row 2:
Persian-type CERAMIC DESIGN; Creamer, 3"; Pot, 4½"; Sugar, 3"
- Set $275.00–300.00
- Creamer $60.00–70.00
- Sugar with Lid $70.00–80.00

Row 3:
SEASCAPE Motif; Creamer, 2½"; Pot, 4"; Sugar, 3½"
- Set $300.00–325.00
- Creamer $60.00–70.00
- Sugar with Lid $70.00–80.00

Row 4:
LANDSCAPE; Creamer, 3"; Pot, 4½"; Sugar, 4"
- Set $250.00–275.00
- Creamer $45.00–55.00
- Sugar with Lid $55.00–65.00

Row 5:
GIBSON GIRLS Motif; Creamer, 3"; Pot, 4½"; Sugar, 4"
- Set $400.00–450.00
- Creamer $75.00–90.00
- Sugar with Lid $100.00–110.00

Plate 71

Creamware

Mark: Generally none.

Plate 71

Row 1:

- PERSIAN Tea Set; Creamer, 3" $75.00–100.00
- PERSIAN Tea Set; Teapot, 4½" $175.00–200.00
- PERSIAN Tea Set; Chocolate Pot, 6½" $200.00–250.00
- PERSIAN Tea Set; Sugar, 4" $75.00–100.00
  (Add $150.00 if set is complete.)

Row 2:

- Stylized Crocus Motif; Creamer, 3" $75.00–100.00
- Stylized Crocus Motif; Sugar, 4½" $75.00–120.00
- Good Night Candlestick, 7" $450.00–500.00
- Pitcher, Blue Ribbon, dainty floral decal, 5" $150.00–175.00

Row 3:

- Pot/Liner, 3½" $125.00–150.00
- Pot/Liner, 4", "Imperial Council Meeting, Rochester, July 11, Syrian, Cincinnati, Ohio" $175.00–225.00
- GREEN TINT Pot/Liner, 4" $75.00–100.00
- Pot/Liner, 3½" $125.00–150.00

Row 4:

- Cherries Motif Teapot, 8½" $600.00–700.00
- Trivet, 6" $300.00–350.00
- Pitcher, floral decal, 8" $250.00–275.00

Plate 72

Gold Traced and Decorated and Gold Traced

Mark: Generally none.

Plate 72

- Candlestick, 9" $100.00–125.00
- Candlestick, 9" $125.00–150.00
- Candlestick, 4", "More light goeth," embossed mark shown above $150.00–175.00
- Candlestick, 9" $150.00–175.00
- Candlestick, 8½" $150.00–175.00

Plate 73

Dutch

Mark: None.

Plate 73

Row 1:

- Shaving Mug, 4" $125.00–150.00
- Pitcher, 7½" $225.00–275.00
- Child's Teapot, 4½" $275.00–350.00

Row 2:

- Pin Tray, 4" $65.00–75.00
- Teapot, 6½" $400.00–450.00
- Toothbrush Holder, 4" $100.00–125.00

Plate 74

Dutch

Mark: None.

Plate 74

Row 1:

- Child's Creamer, 1½" $100.00–125.00
- Child's Teapot, 4" $200.00–250.00
- Child's Sugar, 3" $100.00–125.00

Row 2:

- Child's Soap Dish with lid (shown in stand), 3" $250.00–275.00
- Child's Milk Pitcher, 4½" $250.00–275.00
- Child's Tumbler, 4" $225.00–250.00
- Child's Tumbler, 4" $200.00–225.00

Row 3:

- Humidor, 6", "Compliments of Hotel Olympia, Boston, Massachusetts" $200.00–250.00
- Plate, 11" $100.00–125.00
- Child's Creamer, 3" $175.00–200.00
- Teapot, 7", unusual squeezebag trim $350.00–400.00

Row 4:

- Child's Combinet, 10½" $400.00–450.00
- Child's Potty, 5½" $350.00–400.00
- Tankard, 11½" $175.00–200.00

Plate 75

Creamware

Mark: Generally none.

Plate 75

Row 1:

Mug, 5", "F O E, Liberty Truth, Justice, Equality" $125.00–150.00

Mug, 5", "Our Choice, 1908" $275.00–300.00

Mug, 5", "Should Auld Acquaintance Be Forgot," #3............$275.00–300.00

Mug, 5", "F O E" $125.00–150.00

Row 2:

LANDSCAPE Child's Custard Cup, 2½".$75.00–100.00

Tumbler, 4" $125.00–150.00

DECORATED CERAMIC Jardiniere/Liner, 4"....................$100.00–125.00

DECORATED CERAMIC Jardiniere/Liner, 3½" $100.00–125.00

Mug, 3½", "Susan Swartz, 3-17-28," hand painted, rare $450.00–500.00

Row 3:

Pitcher, 6", Roseville Potter Co., Zanesville, Ohio, red ink stamp..................$325.00–350.00

Coffeepot with hunt scene decal, 10", brown glazed inside, rare..$900.00–1,000.00

CERAMIC DESIGN Teapot, 9" $400.00–450.00

Row 4:

Indian decal Mug, 5" $150.00–175.00

Tankard, 11½"..................................$350.00–400.00

Mug, 5" $150.00–175.00

Mug, 5", "International China, Masonic Temple, Chicago," red ink stamp.$150.00–175.00

Tankard, 11½", "Loyal Order of Moose, Howdy Pap" $200.00–250.00

Mug, 5" $100.00–125.00

Stein Sets

Mark: Generally none.

Plate 76

Row 1:

Mug, 5", floral decal $100.00–125.00

Mug, 5", Wm. Jennings Bryan..................$275.00–300.00

Mug, 5", strawberry decal $125.00–150.00

Row 2:

Mugs, 5", Knights of Pythias, various scenes, each...................$175.00–200.00

Row 3:

Mug, 5", "Englewood Commandery," No. 59 — K.T., 1000 members, Sept. 11th, 1915, J.A. Lozier," Roseville Pottery Co., Zanesville, Ohio, red ink stamp $150.00–175.00

QUAKER MEN Mug, 5"..........................$225.00–275.00

Tankard, 12" $325.00–375.00

Tankard, 12", Elk...............................$200.00–225.00

Mug, 5", no mark $125.00–150.00

Mug, 5", Shrine, "Osman Temple, Feb. 14, 1916................$175.00–200.00

Row 4:

Tankard, 12", "F O E, Liberty, Truth, Justice, Equality" $225.00–275.00

Tankard, 12", K O P, "Friendship" $425.00–475.00

Tankard, 11½", carnation decal..$250.00–300.00

Tankard, 10½", Indian decal..$350.00–400.00

Tankard, 10½", "F O E" $275.00–325.00

Plate 76

Plate 77

Plate 78

Creamware
Mark: Generally none.

Plate 77
Row 1:
- HOLLY Tumbler, 4" $250.00–300.00
- MEDALLION Pitcher, 3½" $100.00–125.00
- MEDALLION Creamer, 3" $75.00–85.00
- Creamer, Greek Key design, 3½" $75.00–85.00
- QUAKER CHILDREN Hair Receiver (no lid), 2" $100.00–125.00
  - with lid $200.00–225.00

Row 2:
- Toothbrush Holder, 5", Lily of the Valley decal $175.00–200.00
- Mug, 5", Wild Rose decal $125.00–150.00
- Mug, 5", Poppy decal $125.00–150.00
- Mug, 5", Mum decal $125.00–150.00

Dog Dishes
Mark: Rv ink stamp over glaze.

Plate 77
Row 3:
- 3" x 8½", 1930s $1,250.00–1,500.00
- 2" x 5½", 1930s, rare size $1,500.00–1,750.00

Watch Fob
Mark: Roseville Pottery, Zanesville, Ohio in red ink.

Plate 78
- 1¾" diameter, "Y" in center signifies Y-Bridge in Zanesville $800.00–900.00

Plate 79

Creamware

Mark: Generally none.

Plate 79

Row 1:

- Ring Tree, 3½", Forget-Me-Not....$125.00–150.00
- Pin Box, 4", yellow ribbon with dainty floral decal....$225.00–250.00
- Cake Plate, 10"....$250.00–275.00
- Candlesticks, 2", each....$150.00–175.00

Row 2:

- Pitcher, 7", decal decoration....$200.00–250.00
- Cuspidor, 10",....$450.00–500.00
- CERAMIC DESIGN, 2 pc. Flower Arranger, 2"....$100.00–125.00

Row 2 (continued):

- 2 pc. Flower Arranger, 2"....$100.00–125.00

Row 3:

- Tankard, 12"....$250.00–300.00
- Mug, 5", "International China Co, Masonic Temple, Chicago" in red ink....$175.00–200.00
- Tankard, 11½"....$325.00–375.00
- Mug, 5"....$175.00–200.00
- Tankard, 11½", Cherry decal....$325.00–375.00

Plate 80

Old Ivory, Ivory Tint
Mark: None.

Plate 80
Compote, 9" $200.00–250.00
Pot, 3½", no liner..........................$95.00–110.00
with liner $150.00–175.00

Creamware
Mark: Generally none.

Plate 81
CERAMIC DESIGN
Persian-type Pot, 8" $225.00–250.00
Plate with Nude, 8" $550.00–650.00
LANDSCAPE
Coffeepot, 10" $450.00–500.00

Plate 81

Plate 82

Holly
Mark: None.

Plate 82
Chamberstick, 7" $600.00–700.00
Teapot, 4½" $350.00–400.00
Creamer, 3"..$200.00–225.00
Reverse side of chamberstick $500.00–600.00

Plate 83

Old Ivory, Ivory Tint

Mark: None.

Plate 83

Row 1:

Planter, 4" $75.00–85.00
Humidor, 6" $225.00–275.00
Double Bud Vase, 5" x 6½" $100.00–125.00

Row 2:

Jardiniere/Liner, 8", #513 .... $250.00–300.00
Tankard, 13½" $300.00–350.00
Jardiniere, 9" $275.00–325.00

Plate 84

Forget-Me-Not

Mark: None.

Plate 84

Sugar, 3" $100.00–125.00
Creamer, 1½" $100.00–125.00

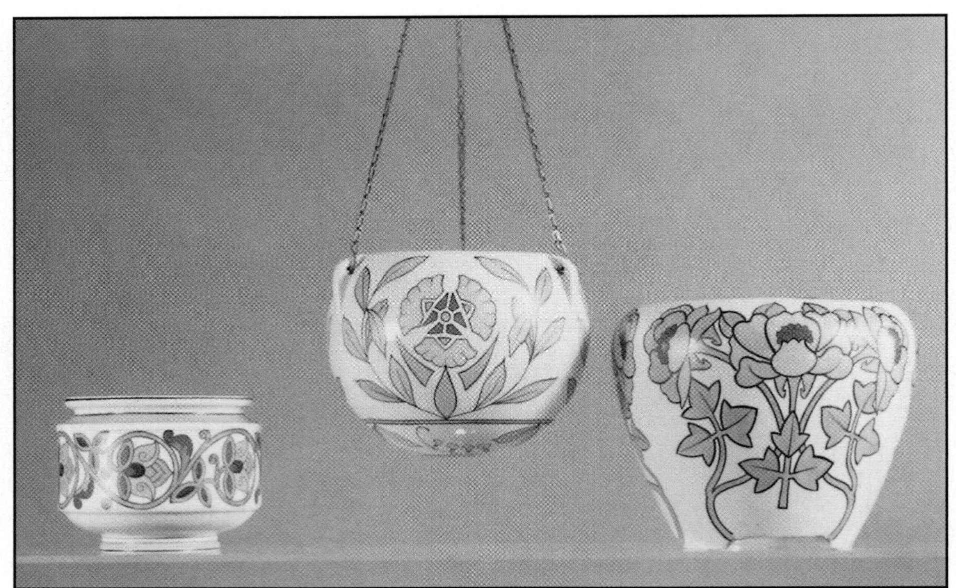

Plate 85

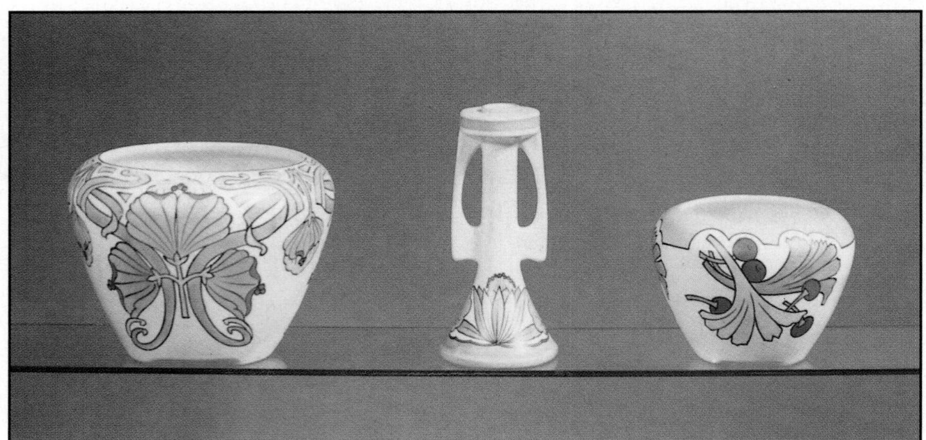

Plate 86

Persian

If marked: Roseville Pottery, Zanesville, Ohio, in red ink.

Plate 85

- Jardiniere, 5", marked in red ink, Roseville Pottery, Zanesville, Ohio..............................$350.00–400.00
- Hanging Basket, 9"..$500.00–600.00
- Jardiniere, 8"..$450.00–500.00

Plate 86

- Jardiniere, 6½", marked in red ink, Roseville Pottery, Zanesville, Ohio, #462-7 incised....................$350.00–400.00
- Candlestick, 8½", Brush-McCoy, Cleo
- Jardiniere, 5"..$250.00–300.00

Plate 87

Plate 88

Blended Glaze

Mark: None.

Plate 87

- Jardiniere, base diameter, 4¼", Pea Pod embossing....................$75.00–100.00
- Jardiniere and Pedestal, 12" overall, Pine Cone decoration....................$200.00–250.00
- Jardiniere, 5½", base diameter....................$100.00–125.00

Ceramic Design

Mark: None.

Plate 88

- Tumblers, 4", each....................$75.00–100.00
- Pitcher, 6½"....................$200.00–250.00

Plate 89

Plate 89
Row 1:
- Cuspidor, 5", no mark $100.00–125.00
- GOLD TRACED Cuspidor, 5" $175.00–200.00
- FERN TRAIL Cuspidor, 5" $125.00–150.00

Row 2:
- MERCIAN Jardiniere, 8", mark below $2,000.00–2,500.00
  A one-of-a-kind piece decorated with decals; hand-lettered mark.
- OLD IVORY Jardiniere, 8" $250.00–300.00

Row 3:
- DECORATED MATT Jardiniere, 9", (CS)..................$2,000.00–2,500.00
- DECORATED MATT Jardiniere, 8", (HR).................$2,000.00–2,500.00

THE ROSEVILLE POTTERY CO
-MERCIAN-
545-8

Plate 90

Venetian

If marked: Venetian impressed; Fire Proof Venetian.

Plate 90
- Bake Pan, 7" $50.00–60.00
- Pudding Crock.......................................$40.00–50.00
- Bake Pan, 9" $55.00–65.00

Plate 91

Pitchers

Plate 91

Row 1:

IDEAL Pitcher, 6½" $125.00–150.00

Bowl, 5½" x 9½", Rv ink stamp $80.00–100.00

IDEAL Pitcher, 6½" $125.00–150.00

Row 2:

Pitcher, 7½"........................$125.00–150.00

Pitcher, 7½"........................$100.00–125.00

Pitcher, 6", Rv ink stamp $100.00–125.00

Pitchers

Plate 92

Row 1:

Bake Pan, 3" x 10", Rv ink stamp under glaze..................$75.00–85.00

Pitcher, 8", Rv ink stamp under glaze.........................$125.00–150.00

Row 2:

Mug, 3½", Rv ink stamp $60.00–70.00

Mug, 4", Rv ink stamp $60.00–70.00

Mug, 5", Rv ink stamp $60.00–70.00

Mug, 6", Rv ink stamp $75.00–85.00

Pitcher, 7½", Rv ink stamp............................$100.00–125.00

Plate 92

Plate 93

Juvenile

If marked: Small Rv ink stamp (may contain shape number in black or red ink).

Plate 93

Row 1:

FAT PUPPY Mug, 3½" $500.00–600.00
FAT PUPPY Pitcher, 3½"...........$500.00–600.00
FAT PUPPY Plate, 7"..................$500.00–600.00
SAD PUPPY Creamer, 3½" $500.00–600.00
SAD PUPPY Bowl, 4½" $500.00–600.00

Row 2:

DUCK WITH BOOTS
Creamer, 3"; hi-gloss* $250.00–300.00
DUCK WITH BOOTS
Bowl, 5"; hi-gloss* $300.00–350.00
CHICKS Rolled-edge Plate,
8"; hi-gloss*........................$400.00–450.00
CHICKS Bowl, 6"; hi-gloss* $350.00–400.00
CHICKS Side Pour Creamer, 3" ..$250.00–275.00

Row 3:

CHICKS Custard, 2½" $350.00–400.00
CHICKS Creamer, 3" $125.00–150.00
CHICKS Small Rolled-edge
Plate, 7" $100.00–125.00
CHICKS Side Pour Pitcher, 3"..$125.00–150.00
CHICKS Bowl, 4½"....................$100.00–125.00
CHICKS Cup, 2";
Saucer, 5½".........................$250.00–300.00

Row 4:

CHICKS Baby's Plate, 8" $100.00–125.00
CHICKS Egg Cup, 3½"..............$200.00–250.00
CHICKS Cake Plate, 9½"...........$600.00–700.00
CHICKS Pudding Dish, 3½" $275.00–300.00
CHICKS Plate, 7".......................$150.00–175.00

* The items marked with the asterisk indicate pieces with wider bands of color. They were introduced in the 1930s and proved unpopular because the color was placed on top of the glossy glaze and quickly wore off. Today mint-condition examples of this kind are very rare. (You may find an occasional matt-glazed example with a band somewhat wider than normal, but unless it has been applied over a glossy glaze, the rarity value does not apply.)

Plate 94

Juvenile

If marked: Small Rv ink stamp (may contain shape number in black or red ink).

Plate 94

Row 1:

- BEAR Creamer, 4" $650.00–700.00
- BEAR Bowl, 6" $700.00–750.00
- BEAR Mug, 3½" $700.00–750.00

Row 2:

- GOOSE Cup, 2"; Saucer, 5½" $900.00–1,000.00
- GOOSE Teapot, 4" $1,500.00–1,750.00
- GOOSE Sugar, 3" $600.00–700.00

Row 3:

- GOOSE Mug, 3½" $500.00–550.00
- GOOSE Plate, 7" $500.00–550.00
- GOOSE Creamer, 4" $500.00–550.00
- GOOSE Custard, 2½" $600.00–650.00

Row 4:

- RABBIT Custard, 2½" $250.00–300.00
- RABBIT set, Side Pour Pitcher, 3" $150.00–175.00
- RABBIT set, Bowl, 4½" $125.00–150.00
- RABBIT Creamer, 3½" $125.00–150.00
- RABBIT Cup, 2"; Saucer, 5" $200.00–250.00
- RABBIT Pudding Dish, 1½" x 3½" $250.00–275.00

Row 5:

- RABBIT Egg Cup, 3", rare $600.00–700.00
- RABBIT Baby's Plate, 7" $100.00–125.00
- RABBIT Baby's Plate, 8" $100.00–125.00
- RABBIT Plate, 7" $125.00–150.00
- RABBIT Egg Cup, 3½" $250.00–300.00

ROSEVILLE POTTERY INC.
ZANESVILLE, OHIO

No. 1 JUVENILE SET

Three Piece Set Contains:

No. 1 – 3" Mug – Blue band with Duck decoration

No. 2 – 6" Bowl – Pink band with Dog decoration

No. 3 – 7" Plate – Green band with Rabbit decoration

Packed in attractive gift box

WHOLESALE PRICE

$2.50 PER SET
(Box Included)

F.O.B. Zanesville

749

Plate 95

Juvenile

If marked: Small Rv ink stamp (may contain shape number in black or red ink).

Plate 95

RABBIT Pitcher, 7½"..$1,500.00–2,000.00
RABBIT Bowl, 10½"..$800.00–1,000.00

Juvenile

If marked: Small Rv ink stamp (may contain shape number in black or red ink).

Plate 96
Row 1:

CHICKS Creamer, 3"........................$500.00–600.00
CHICKS Teapot, 5", #8........................$800.00–900.00
CHICKS Sugar, 4"........................$600.00–700.00
(Matched set: $2,000.00 – 2,500.00)

Baby Bunting

Plate 96
Rows 2 & 3:

Rolled-edge Plates,
8", each........................$200.00–250.00

Plate 96

Juvenile

If marked: Small Rv ink stamp (may contain shape number in black or red ink).

Plate 97

Plate 97

Row 1:

- SKINNY PUPPY 2-handled Mug, 3" $250.00–275.00
- SKINNY PUPPY Rolled-edge Plate, 8" $125.00–150.00
- SKINNY PUPPY Cup, 2"; Saucer, 5" $200.00–250.00
- SKINNY PUPPY Plate, 8" $125.00–150.00
- SKINNY PUPPY Creamer, 3½" ... $125.00–150.00

Row 2:

- DUCK WITH HAT Creamer, 3½" $100.00–125.00
- DUCK WITH HAT Cup, 2"; Saucer, 3" $200.00–225.00
- DUCK WITH HAT Rolled-edge Plate, 8" $125.00–150.00
- DUCK WITH HAT Plate, 8" $125.00–150.00
- DUCK WITH HAT 2-handled Mug, 3" $200.00–225.00
- DUCK WITH HAT Mug, 3" $100.00–125.00

Row 3:

- SUNBONNET GIRL Creamer, 3½" $125.00–150.00
- SUNBONNET GIRL Cup, 2"; Saucer, 3" $250.00–275.00
- SUNBONNET GIRL Rolled-edge Plate, 8" $150.00–175.00
- SUNBONNET GIRL Plate, 8" $150.00–175.00
- *SUNBONNET GIRL Egg Cup, 4", rare $2,000.00–2,500.00
- SUNBONNET GIRL 2-handled Mug, 3" $275.00–300.00

Row 4:

- Experimental Mug, 3"; Vitro #1237 .... $400.00–500.00
- Boxed Set $1,000.00–1,200.00
- RABBIT Potty, 3" x 6" .... $250.00–300.00 (add $500.00 for lid)

* Except for the Potty in Row 4, all examples on this page are in the high-gloss finish.

Plate 98

Juvenile

If marked: Small Rv ink stamp (may contain shape number in black or red ink).

Plate 98

Row 1:

Nursery Rhyme motif: Set: 3" sugar bowl, 6" teapot, and 3" creamer, rare, 3 pieces w/lids..........................$3,500.00–4,000.00

Row 2:

SANTA CLAUS Creamer, 3½"..................$1,000.00–1,250.00
SANTA CLAUS Rolled-edge Plate, 8".......$1,250.00–1,500.00
SANTA CLAUS Cup, 2"; Saucer, 5"..........$1,500.00–2,000.00

Row 3:

RABBIT Mug, 3"..$175.00–200.00
RABBIT Rolled-edge Plate, 8".........................$200.00–225.00
WB RABBIT Egg Cup, 4", rare.................$2,000.00–2,500.00

Row 4:

WB PIG Plate, 8"......................................$1,750.00–2,000.00
WB PIG Creamer, 4".................................$1,250.00–1,500.00
ROOSTER Plate, 8", series of numbers indicating an experimental, rare............................$3,000.00–4,000.00

Row 5:

Divided Plate, rare, 8½" $1,500.00–1,750.00
WB FANCY CAT Rolled-edge Plate, 8" $2,250.00–2,500.00
WB FANCY CAT Plate, 8".....................$2,250.00–2,500.00
WB FANCY CAT Mug, 3" $1,750.00–2,000.00

Except for the tea set in Row 1, all examples on this page are in the high-gloss finish.
(WB) Wide Band examples are rarer than narrow bars.

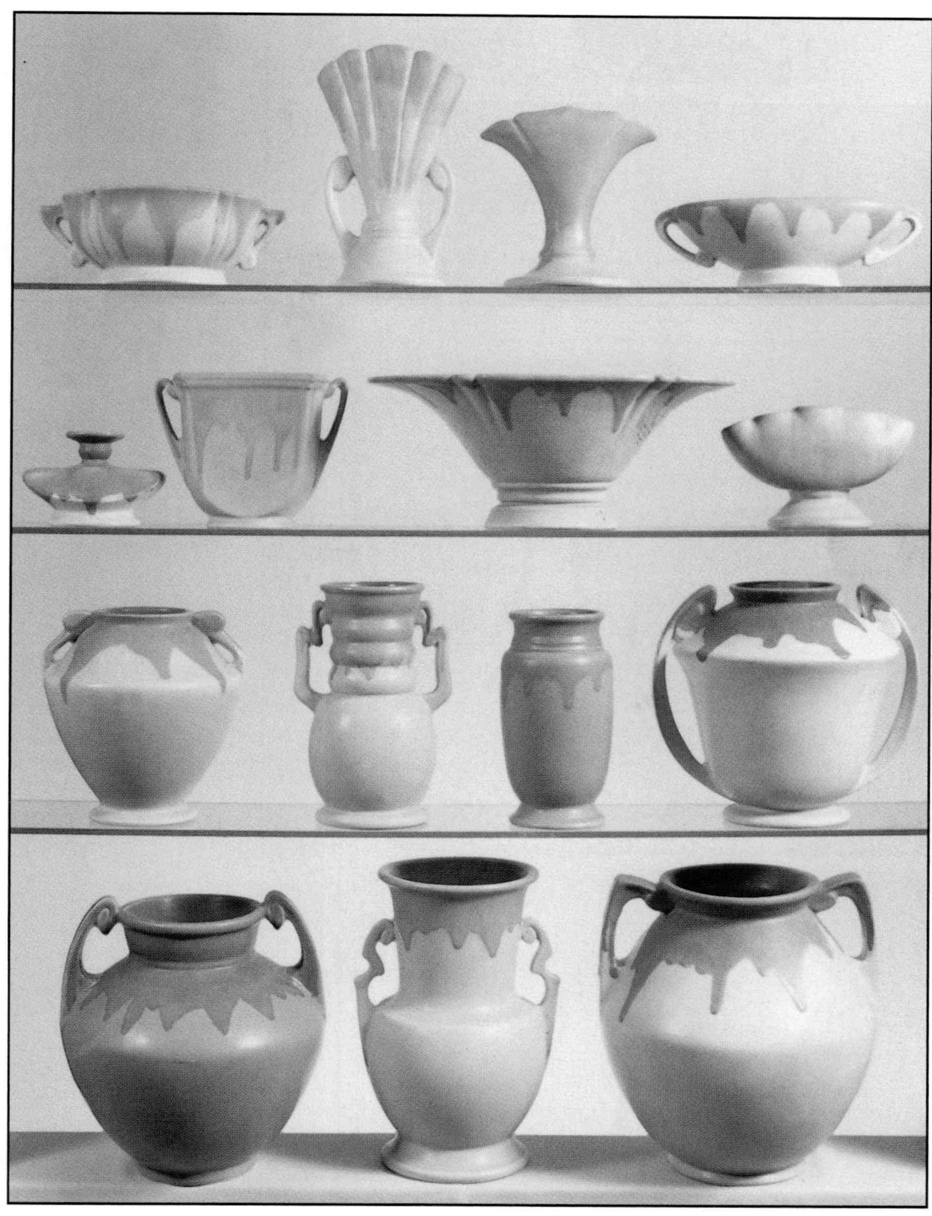

Plate 99

Carnelian I

Marks: Large Rv ink stamp; paper sticker.

Plate 99

Row 1:
- Bowl/Frog, 3" x 8½" $90.00–100.00
- Vase, 8" $100.00–125.00
- Fan Vase, 6" $70.00–80.00
- Bowl, 3" x 9" $80.00–90.00

Row 2:
- Candle Holder/Frog, 3½" $70.00–80.00
- Pillow Vase, 5" $90.00–100.00
- Center Bowl, 5" x 12½" $125.00–150.00
- Flower Frog, 4½" $75.00–85.00

Row 3:
- Vase, 7" $125.00–150.00
- Vase, 8" $125.00–150.00
- Vase, 7" $100.00–125.00
- Vase, 8" $150.00–200.00

Row 4:
- Vase, 9½" $200.00–250.00
- Vase, 10" $200.00–250.00
- Vase, 10" $200.00–250.00

Plate 100

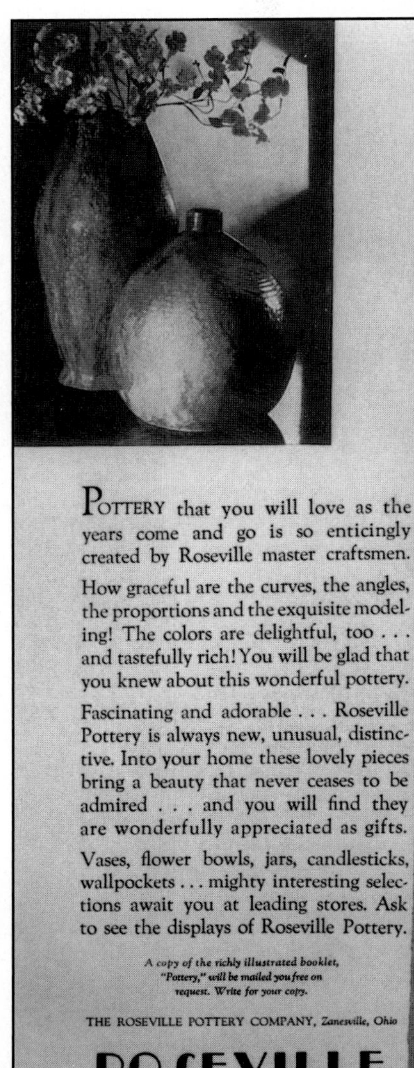

Carnelian II

Marks: Large Rv ink stamp; paper sticker; rarely, foil sticker.

Plate 100

Row 1:
- Vase, 5" $225.00–275.00
- Vase, 7" $225.00–275.00
- Planter, 3" x 8" $125.00–150.00

Row 2:
- Vase, 8" $375.00–425.00
- Vase, 6" $375.00–425.00
- Vase, 8" $375.00–425.00

Row 3:
- Vase, 7" $200.00–225.00
- Ewer, 12½" $800.00–900.00
- Vase, 10" $225.00–275.00
- Vase, 8" $225.00–275.00

Carnelian II

Marks: Large Rv ink stamp; paper sticker; rarely, foil sticker.

Plate 101
Row 1:
Vase, 12", rare shape..........................$1,500.00–1,750.00
Vase, 15", rare shape..........................$1,750.00–2,000.00
Vase, 12", rare shape..........................$1,250.00–1,500.00

Row 2:
Vase, 12"..$1,250.00–1,500.00
Lamp Base, 8"..$700.00–800.00
Vase, 14"..$800.00–900.00

Plate 101

Plate 102

Carnelian II

Marks: Large Rv ink stamp; paper sticker; rarely, foil sticker.

Plate 102
Vase, 18½"..$2,500.00–3,000.00
Vase, 14½"..$2,000.00–2,500.00

Plate 103

Carnelian II

Marks: Large Rv ink stamp; paper sticker; rarely, foil sticker.

Plate 103

Row 1:

- Vase, 8"......$200.00–250.00
- Basket, 4" x 10"......$225.00–275.00
- Vase, 7"......$175.00–200.00

Row 2:

- Bowl, 3" x 8"......$125.00–150.00
- Bowl, 5" x 12½"......$275.00–300.00
- Fan Vase, 6½"......$125.00–150.00

Row 3:

- Bowl, 4" x 10"......$225.00–275.00
- Bowl, 4" x 15"......$325.00–375.00

Row 4:

- Vase, 9"......$225.00–275.00
- Vase, 9"......$225.00–275.00
- Vase, 8"......$325.00–375.00
- Frog, 4" x 6"......$125.00–175.00

Mostique

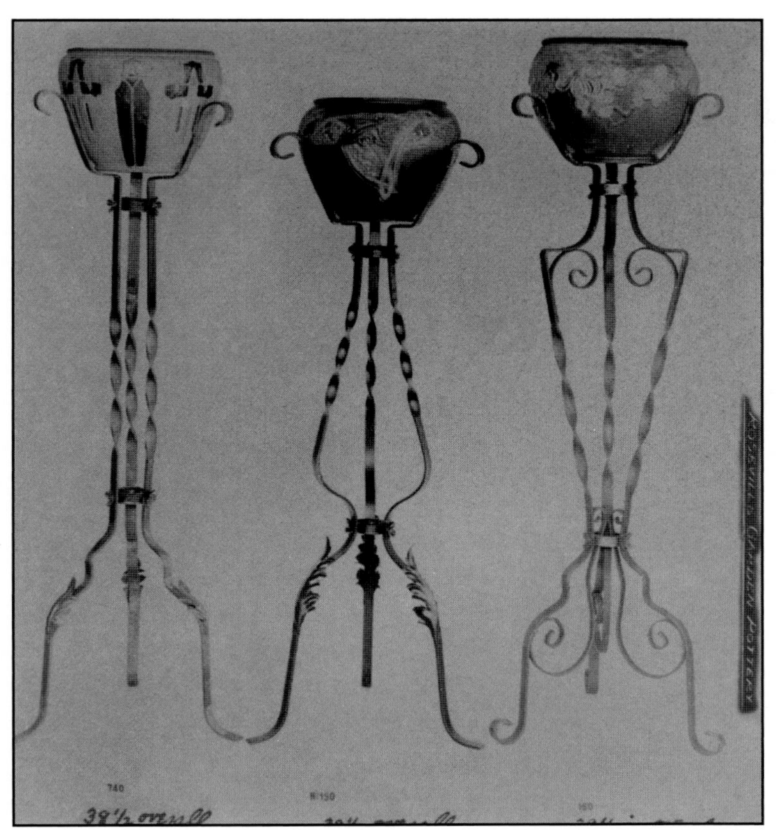

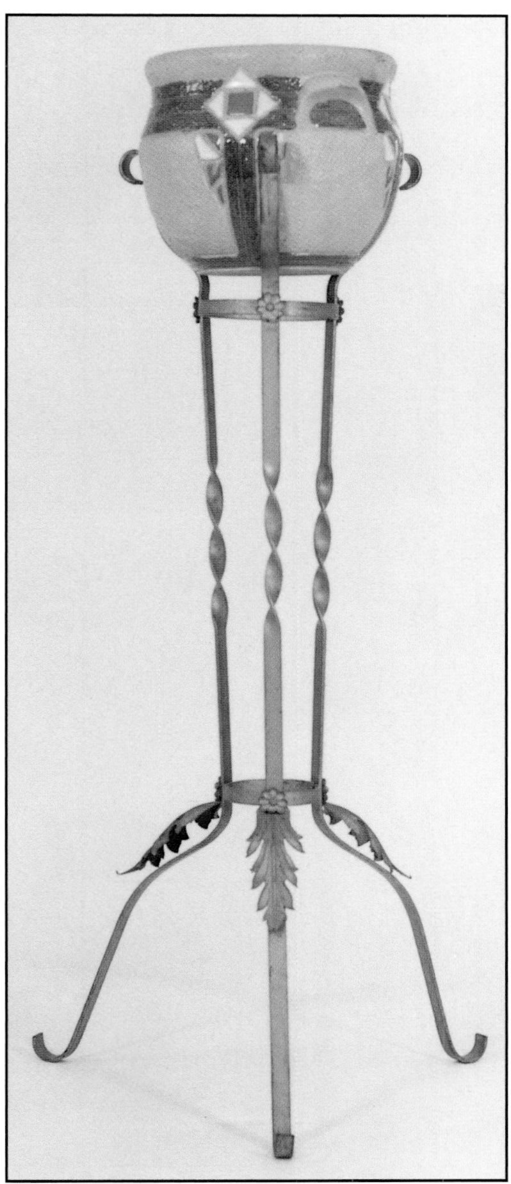

Plate 104

Mostique

If marked: Rv ink stamp; on rare occasion, MOSTIQUE.

Plate 104
Jardiniere, 10"......................$900.00–1,000.00
Metal Stand, 38" $200.00–250.00

Plate 105

Mostique

If marked: Rv ink stamp; on rare occasion, MOSTIQUE.

Plate 105

Row 1:
- Hanging Basket, 7" $350.00–400.00
- Bowl, 7" $125.00–150.00
- Bowl, 7" $125.00–150.00
- Bowl, 5½" $100.00–125.00

Row 2:
- Bowl, 9½" $175.00–200.00
- Compote, 7" $300.00–350.00

Row 2 (continued):
- Bowl, 9" $300.00–350.00

Row 3:
- Vase, 10" $400.00–500.00
- Vase, 12" $750.00–850.00
- Jardiniere, 8" $225.00–250.00
- Vase, 6" $150.00–200.00

Plate 106

Rosecraft Panel

Mark: Rv ink stamp.

Plate 106

Row 1:

Item	Brown	Green	Red
Vase, 6"	$175.00–200.00	$225.00–250.00	
Covered Jar, 10"	$550.00–600.00	$750.00–850.00	
Bowl Vase, 4"	$200.00–225.00	$250.00–275.00	

Row 2:

Item	Brown	Green	Red
Nude Lamp Base, 10"	$1,500.00–1,750.00	$1,750.00–2,000.00	$3,000.00–3,250.00
Window Box, 6" x 12"	$450.00–500.00	$550.00–600.00	
Vase, 10"	$400.00–450.00	$550.00–600.00	

Plate 107

Imperial I

Mark: None.

Plate 107

Row 1:

- Basket, 9", #7 .... $200.00–250.00
- Basket, 10", #8 .... $250.00–300.00
- Basket, 10", #9 .... $250.00–300.00
- Vase, 8" $175.00–225.00

Row 2:

- Vase, 10" $250.00–300.00

Row 2 (continued):

- Compote, 6½" $175.00–225.00
- Vase, 8" $225.00–275.00

Row 3:

- Vase, 10" $250.00–300.00
- Planter, 14" x 16" $300.00–350.00
- Vase, 12" $300.00–350.00

Velmoss Scroll

Plate 108

Velmoss Scroll*

Mark: None.

Plate 108

Row 1:

- Vase, 5" $125.00–150.00
- Vase, 8" $175.00–200.00
- Bowl, 3", C7 .... $100.00–125.00

Row 2:

- Vase, 8" $150.00–175.00
- Vase, 10" $150.00–175.00
- Vase, 12" $350.00–400.00
- Vase, 10" $200.00–250.00

*This line name remains under investigation.

Collectors have been studying this line for decades, speculating about but unsure of which Ohio pottery might have been its manufacturer. Most ruled out Roseville because it seemed illogical that they would have produced a line so similar to Donatello. Weller made Fairfield, so nearly like this line that Weller seemed an unlikely candidate as well. Though Brush-McCoy appeared to be the next logical choice, the Sanfords' in-depth research of that company's lines of production eliminated that possibility. Several pieces of this ware surfaced over the years; none was ever marked. But the glaze looked like a finish that Roseville had used on some creamware; and as collectors began to network, reports of shapes common to many of Roseville's lines began to suggest Roseville more strongly — in particular, a double bud vase. Only they produced double bud vases with short, thick receptacles that almost look like candle holders. Flowerpots, hanging baskets, wall pockets, bowls, jardiniere and pedestal sets, baskets, a window box, an ashtray, and several vases surfaced. Though the other Ohio potteries made some of these shapes, only Roseville consistently made all of them from line to line. When the jardiniere in Plate 109 (with the unusual glaze) was found with a shape number carved into the bottom, all the clues fell into place. The 500 series numbers were used on many jardinieres in the 1916 – 1920 timeline. The number on the jardiniere was #584, a previously missing/unknown number in the jardiniere series. Roseville scholars believe this line was a predecessor to Donatello, made ca. 1915 – 1918, when most Roseville products were unmarked. Because of the number of pieces that have been found, they regard it as a valid production line rather than experimental. It may have been an extension of the very limited Cameo line, possibly one of their first entries into what was eventually dubbed Industrial Artware. (The name Cameo II is of course unofficial.)

Plate 109

Cameo II

Mark: None.

Plate 109

Row 1:

Jardiniere, 8" high $375.00–450.00

Row 2:

Jardiniere, 9" high $450.00–550.00

Jardiniere, 9" high, unusual color $550.00–650.00

Plate 110

Cameo II

Mark: None.

Plate 110

Row 1:

- Double Bud Vase, 4" x 7½" $200.00–250.00
- Flowerpot, 5½" $200.00–250.00

Row 2:

- Vase, 7½" $275.00–325.00
- Vase, 7½" $300.00–350.00

Row 3:

- Wall Pocket, 9½" $250.00–300.00
- Jardiniere, 9" high, unusual color $550.00–650.00

Plate 111

Plate 112

Donatello

If marked: Large Rv ink stamp; impressed Donatello, RPCo; or dark blue shape numbers.

Plate 111

Row 1:

- Powder Jar, 2" x 5" $400.00–450.00
- Vase, 6", rare matt glaze $350.00–400.00
- Double Bud Vase, 7", rare matt glaze....................$350.00–400.00
- Incense Burner, 3½" $450.00–500.00

Row 2:

- Vase, 8½", unusual gray coloring....................$350.00–400.00
- Vase, 12"....................$300.00–350.00
- Vase, 9½" $225.00–275.00
- Plate, 8"....................$400.00–450.00

Plate 112

Top:

- Metal stencil, 16½" x 3", was used to letter packing crates....................$400.00–500.00

Bottom:

- Light sconce, 18" x 6", made by the Roseville Pottery for the Rogge Hotel in Zanesville, now demolished. $4,000.00–5,000.00

Plate 113

Donatello

If marked: Large Rv ink stamp; impressed Donatello, RPCo; or dark blue shape numbers.

Plate 113

Row 1:

- Bowl, 6" $60.00–75.00
- Ashtray, 3" $125.00–175.00
- Hanging Basket, 7" $200.00–250.00
- Ashtray, 3" $125.00–175.00
- Ashtray, 2", rare matt glaze $175.00–225.00

Row 2:

- Rolled-edge Bowl, 9½" $100.00–125.00
- Bowl, 8½" x 3½", #238/7 ....$100.00–125.00
- Bowl, 8" x 3" $100.00–125.00

Row 3:

- Cuspidor, 5½" $250.00–300.00
- Jardiniere, 6" $125.00–150.00
- Compote, 5" $100.00–125.00
- Candlestick, 6½" $150.00–175.00

Row 4:

- Vase, 8" $80.00–95.00
- Vase, 10" $100.00–125.00
- Vase, 12" $125.00–175.00
- Compote, 9½" $150.00–175.00
- Basket, 7½" $300.00–350.00

Plate 114

Rozane (1917)

If marked: Roseville Pottery Rozane ink stamp in black, brown, or blue.

Plate 114

Row 1:
- Bowl, 3", green glaze $100.00–125.00
- Compote, 8" $150.00–175.00
- Vase, 6½", pink glaze $100.00–125.00

Row 2:
- Urn, 6½" $175.00–200.00
- Footed Bowl, 5" $175.00–200.00
- Bowl, 3½" $100.00–125.00

Row 3:
- Bowl, 5" $125.00–150.00

Row 3 (continued):
- Compote, 6½" $150.00–175.00
- Bowl, 4½" $125.00–150.00

Row 4:
- Basket, 11", blue glaze $300.00–350.00
- Vase, 8" $150.00–175.00
- Vase, 10", green glaze $200.00–250.00
- Vase, 10", yellow glaze $200.00–250.00
- Vase, 8" $150.00–175.00

Plate 115

Azurine, Orchid, and Turquoise

Mark: Paper sticker.

Plate 115

Bud Vases, 10", pair $100.00–150.00
Console Bowl, 12½"................................$75.00–100.00

Plate 116

Double Bud Vase, 5" x 8" $125.00–150.00
Vase, 10" $150.00–175.00
Vase, 8" $75.00–100.00

Plate 116

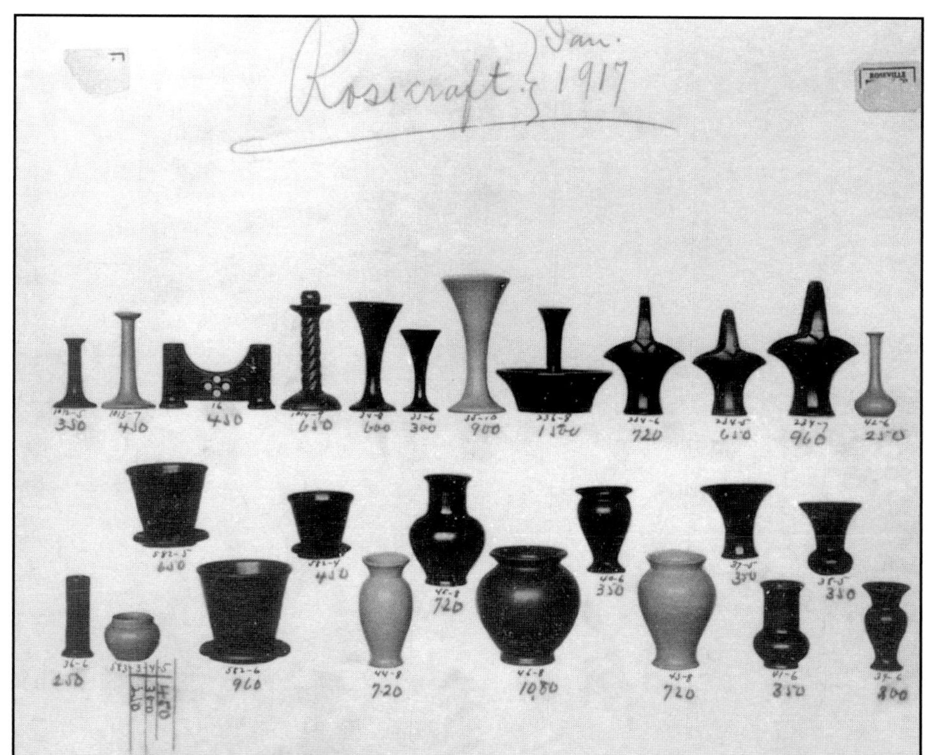

Compare shapes with those of Rosecraft Blended in Plate 117.

Plate 117

Rosecraft Blended

Mark: None.

Plate 117

Row 1:

- Vase, 6" $90.00–110.00
- Window Box, 5" x 8", with separate Frog $125.00–150.00
- Jardiniere, 4" $90.00–110.00
- Bud Vase, #36–6 .... $90.00–110.00

Row 2:

- Vase, 10", #35 .... $125.00–150.00
- Vase, 8" $150.00–175.00
- Vase, 12½" $150.00–175.00

Lombardy

Mark: Paper sticker.

Plate 118

- Jardiniere, 6½" $150.00–200.00
- Vase, 6" $150.00–200.00

Plate 118

Plate 119

Rosecraft Black and Colors

Marks: Foil and paper stickers; Rv ink stamp (on colors).

Plate 119

Row 1:
- Compote, 4" x 11"....................$125.00–150.00

Row 2:
- Bowl, 3" x 8"....................$75.00–95.00
- Double Bud Vase, 5"....................$125.00–150.00
- Bowl/Frog, 2" x 8½"....................$75.00–95.00

Row 3:
- Bowl, 5"....................$125.00–150.00
- Ginger Jar, 8"....................$250.00–300.00

Row 3 (continued):
- Bud Vase, 8"....................$75.00–95.00
- Flowerpot, 4½"....................$150.00–175.00

Row 4:
- Vase, 10"....................$175.00–200.00
- Vase, 13½"....................$200.00–250.00
- Vase, 10"....................$175.00–200.00
- Vase, 9"....................$175.00–200.00

Plate 120

Rosecraft Vintage

Mark: Rv ink stamp.

Plate 120

Row 1:

- Bowl, 3" $100.00–125.00
- Vase, 6" $200.00–250.00
- Vase, 4" $150.00–175.00

Row 2:

- Vase, 8½" $350.00–400.00
- Window Box, 6" x 11½" $500.00–550.00
- Vase, 12" $500.00–550.00

Plate 121

Rosecraft Hexagon

Mark: Rv ink stamp.

Plate 121

Row 1:

Item	Brown	Green	Blue
Vase, 6"	$275.00–325.00	$375.00–425.00	$475.00–525.00
Vase, 5"	$225.00–275.00	$325.00–375.00	$425.00–475.00
Vase, 5", rare, blue hi-gloss glaze			$425.00–525.00
Vase, 4"	$200.00–250.00	$300.00–350.00	$400.00–450.00
Bowl, 7½"	$175.00–200.00	$275.00–300.00	$375.00–400.00

Row 2:

Item	Brown	Green	Blue
Candlestick, 8", each	$375.00–425.00	$475.00–525.00	$575.00–625.00
Vase, 8"	$375.00–425.00	$475.00–525.00	$575.00–625.00
Double Bud Vase, 5"	$375.00–425.00	$475.00–525.00	$575.00–625.00
Vase, 8"	$375.00–425.00	$475.00–525.00	$575.00–625.00
Candlestick, 8", each	$375.00–425.00	$475.00–525.00	$575.00–625.00

Plate 122

Plate 123

Lustre

If marked: Paper sticker; Rv impressed.

Plate 122

Row 1:

Basket, 10" $200.00–250.00
Basket, 6" $200.00–250.00

Row 2:

Bowl, 5" $95.00–125.00
Vase, 12" $200.00–250.00
Candlestick, 10", each $100.00–125.00
Candlestick, 5½", each $45.00–55.00

Plate 123

Vase, 12" $200.00–250.00
Basket, 6½" $175.00–200.00

Plate 124

Plate 125

Matt Color

If marked: Paper and foil stickers.

Plate 124

Bowl, 3", #15 .... $70.00–80.00
Vase, 4" $70.00–80.00
Bowl, 4" $70.00–80.00
Vase, 4" $70.00–80.00
Pot, 4" $70.00–80.00

Imperial II

If marked: Paper sticker.

Plate 125

Vase, 9", #475 .... $1,250.00–1,500.00
Vase, 9½", #477 .... $1,250.00–1,500.00
Vase, 8", #476 .... $1,750.00–2,000.00
Vase, 7½", #473 .... $1,500.00–1,750.00

Plate 126

Imperial II

If marked: Paper sticker.

Plate 126

Row 1:

- Bowl, 4½", #198 .... $350.00–400.00
- Vase, 5", #468 .... $250.00–300.00
- Vase, 6", #469 .... $350.00–400.00
- Vase, 4½", #200 .... $300.00–350.00
- Vase, 6", #470 .... $1,250.00–1,500.00

Row 2:

- Bowl, 4", #201 .... $400.00–450.00
- Vase, 5", #467 .... $400.00–450.00
- Bowl, 5" x 8", #206 .... $1,750.00–2,000.00
- Vase, 5", #203 trial glaze $1,750.00–2,000.00

Row 3:

- Vase, 7", #471 .... $550.00–650.00
- Vase, 4", #466 .... $550.00–650.00
- Bowl, 5" x 12½", #207 .... $500.00–550.00
- Vase, 7", #474 .... $400.00–450.00

Row 4:

- Vase, 8", #479 .... $1,250.00–1,500.00
- Vase, 8", #478 .... $550.00–650.00
- Vase, 11", #484 .... $1,750.00–2,000.00
- Vase, 8½", #481 .... $1,250.00–1,500.00

Plate 127

Dogwood I

Mark: None.

Plate 127

Row 1:

Double Bud Vase, 8"....................$175.00–200.00

Tub, 4" x 7"....................$150.00–175.00

Row 2:

Window Box/Liner, 5½" x 13½"....................$400.00–450.00

Vase, 14½", #140....................$700.00–750.00

Dogwood II

Mark: Rv ink stamp.

Plate 128

Row 1:

Vase, 7", #301....................$200.00–250.00

Hanging Basket, 5", #340......$250.00–300.00

Bowl, 6", #150....................$125.00–150.00

Row 2:

Bowl, 4", #151....................$125.00–150.00

Jardiniere, 6", #608.............$150.00–175.00

Jardiniere, 8", #608.............$250.00–300.00

Plate 128

Plate 129

Dahlrose

If marked: Paper sticker.

Plate 129

Row 1:

- Vase, 6", #418 .... $150.00–175.00
- Hanging Basket, 7½", #343 .... $250.00–300.00
- Pillow Vase, 5" x 7", #419 .... $250.00–275.00

Row 2:

- Candlesticks, 3½", #1069, pair $175.00–225.00
- Vase, 6", #364 .... $200.00–250.00
- Bowl Vase, 4", #420 .... $150.00–175.00

Row 3:

- Vase, 8", #366 .... $225.00–275.00

Row 3 (continued):

- Window Box, 6" x 12½", #377 .... $450.00–500.00
- Bud Vase, 8", #78 .... $175.00–225.00

Row 4:

- Window Box, 6" x 16", takes ceramic liner, #375-14 .... $375.00–425.00
- Window Box, 6" x 11½", takes ceramic liner, #375-10 .... $325.00–375.00

Cremona

Cremona

If marked: Paper sticker.

Plate 130

Urn, 4", #351 ....$150.00–175.00
Fan Vase, 5", #73..............................$125.00–150.00
Vase, 8", #356 ....$200.00–250.00
Vase, 12", #361 ....$350.00–400.00

Plate 130

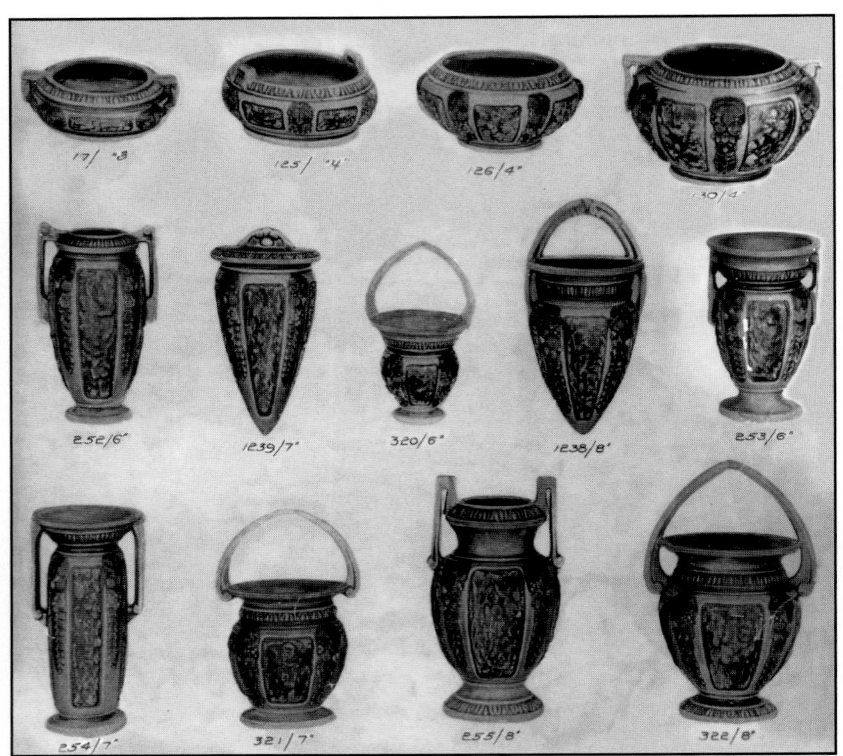

Florentine

Florentine

Plate 131

Florentine

Mark: Rv ink stamp.

Plate 131

Row 1:

- Hanging Basket, 9", #337-7 .... $200.00–250.00
- Jardiniere, 5", #602-5 .... $125.00–150.00
- Ashtray, 5", #17-3 .... $125.00–150.00
- Vase, 8", #255-8 .... $150.00–175.00

Row 2:

- Bowl, 6", #258-5 .... $85.00–100.00
- Bowl, 9", #257-8 .... $85.00–100.00
- Bowl, 7", #125-6 .... $85.00–100.00

Row 3:

- Candlestick, 10½", each, #1050-10 .... $125.00–150.00
- Candlestick, 8½", each, #1049-8 .... $100.00–125.00
- Lamp Base, 8", #750-7 .... $400.00–500.00
- Vase, 7", #254-7 .... $175.00–225.00
- Double Bud Vase, 4½", #41-6 .... $100.00–125.00

Row 4:

- Jardiniere, 8" high, #602-8 .... $200.00–250.00
- Window Box, 11½" $300.00–350.00

Plate 132

Vista

If marked: Rv ink stamp; generally none.

Plate 132

Row 1:

- Basket, 12" $1,500.00–1,750.00
- Vase, 10", #127..$750.00–850.00
- Basket, 9½" $900.00–1,000.00

Row 2:

- Vase, 15", #121–15...$1,000.00–1,200.00
- Vase, 18", #134–18...$2,000.00–2,500.00
- Vase, 18", #131–18...$1,750.00–2,000.00

Plate 133

Victorian Art Pottery

If marked: Rv ink stamp; generally none.

Plate 133

Row 1:

Vase, 7", #257......$500.00–550.00

Urn, 4", #132......$350.00–400.00

Row 2:

Vase, 6", #256......$400.00–450.00

Vase, 8", #260......$550.00–600.00

Vase, 7", #258......$500.00–550.00

Plate 134

Covered Jar, 8", unusual glossy glaze, #261......$600.00–700.00

Plate 134

Plate 135

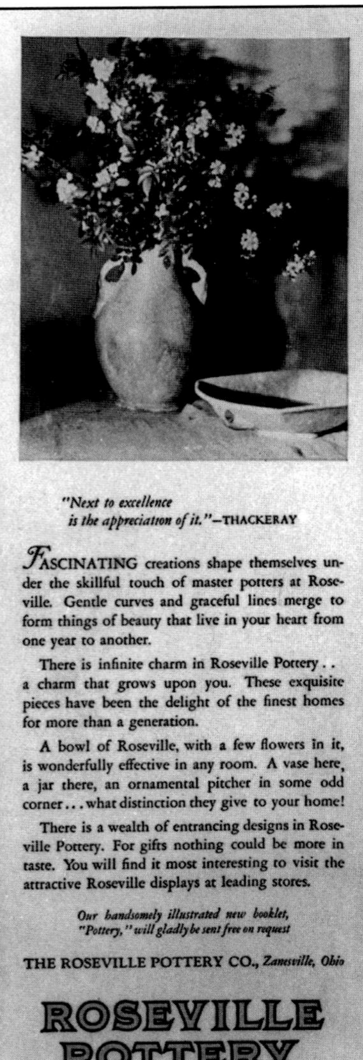

Tuscany

If marked: Paper sticker.

Plate 135

Row 1:

Item	Color	Price	Color	Price
Vase, 4", #68	Pink	$100.00–125.00	Gray/Lt. Blue	$75.00–100.00
Vase, 6", #71	Pink	$125.00–150.00	Gray/Lt. Blue	$100.00–125.00
Flower Arranger, 5", #66	Pink	$100.00–125.00	Gray/Lt. Blue	$75.00–100.00

Row 2:

Item	Color	Price	Color	Price
Vase, 6", #342	Pink	$125.00–150.00	Gray/Lt. Blue	$100.00–125.00
Vase, 9", #346	Pink	$200.00–225.00	Gray/Lt. Blue	$150.00–175.00
Vase, 12", #349	Pink	$300.00–350.00	Gray/Lt. Blue	$225.00–250.00

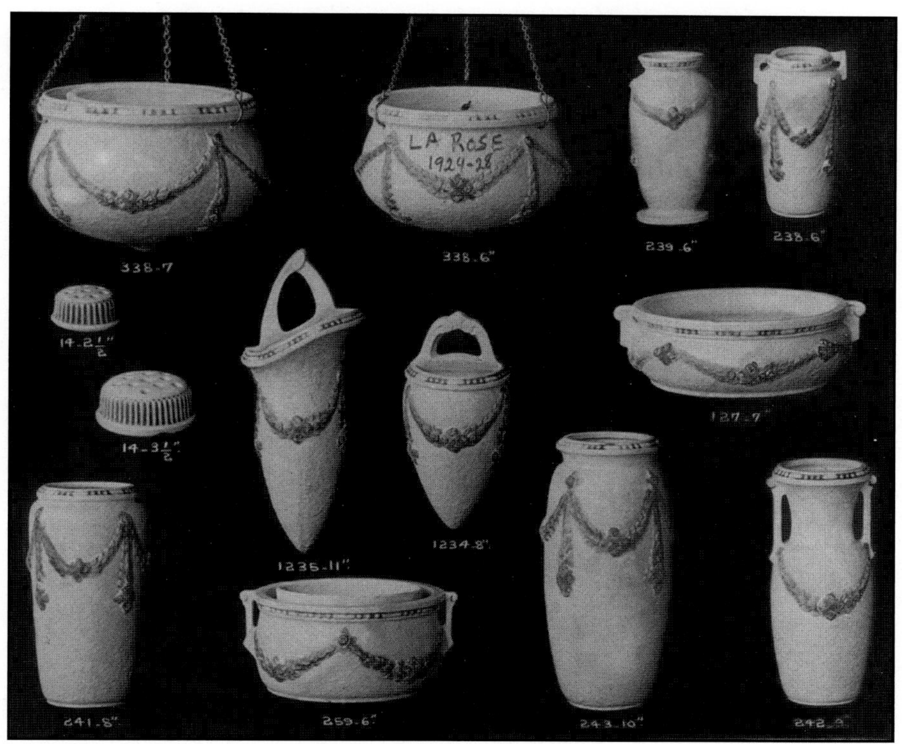

La Rose

Plate 136

La Rose

Mark: Rv ink stamp.

Plate 136
Row 1:

Vase, 4", #236....................................$125.00–150.00
Bowl, 6", #128....................................$125.00–150.00

Row 2:

Wall Pocket, 9", #1233 ....$300.00–350.00
Jardiniere, 6½", #604 ....$150.00–175.00
Vase, 6", #238....................................$150.00–175.00

Volpato

If marked: Rv impressed; paper sticker.

Plate 137

Row 1:

Covered Urn, 8", #3 .... $300.00–350.00

Row 2:

Candlesticks, 9½", pair, #1042 .... $250.00–275.00

Vase, 12", #192 .... $250.00–300.00

Plate 138

Row 1:

Window Box, 2½" x 9" $60.00–75.00

Flowerpot/Saucer, 6" $100.00–125.00

Vase, 9" $100.00–125.00

Candlestick, 10", pair $125.00–150.00

Plate 137

Plate 138

Corinthian

If marked: Rv ink stamp.

Plate 139

Vase, 8", #218 ....$100.00–125.00
Jardiniere, 7", #601 ....$125.00–150.00

Plate 140

Row 1:

Wall Pocket, 8", #1232 ....$200.00–250.00
Hanging Basket, 8", #336 ....$200.00–250.00
Wall Pocket, 10", #1228...$200.00–250.00

Row 2:

Footed Bowl, 4½", #256 ....$100.00–125.00
Vase, 6", #214 ....$125.00–150.00
Vase, 7", #215 ....$100.00–125.00
Bowl, 5", #121 ....$60.00–75.00

Plate 139

Plate 140

Plate 141

Normandy

If marked: Paper sticker; generally none.

Plate 141

Hanging Basket, 7"..$250.00-300.00

Florane

Mark: Rv ink stamp.

Plate 142

Bowl, 5"..$100.00–125.00
Vase, 12½",..$200.00–250.00
Basket, 8½"...$200.00–250.00
Double Bud Vase, 5" $100.00–125.00

Plate 142

Plate 143

Cherry Blossom

If marked: Foil sticker.

Plate 143

Hanging Basket, 8", #350

Brown $400.00–500.00

Pink/blue $2,000.00–2,250.00

Cherry Blossom

Plate 144

Russco

If marked: Foil sticker.

Plate 144

Row 1:

Vase, 8", note heavy crystals, penciled notation on bottom: #61-183, overfired, #696 ....$250.00–275.00

Vase, 7", heavy crystals, #694 ....$175.00–200.00

Row 2:

Double Bud Vase, 8½", #101 ....$100.00–125.00

Vase, 9½", #699 ....$150.00–175.00

Row 2 (continued):

Vase, 8½", #109 ....$125.00–150.00

Row 3:

Vase, 7", heavy crystals, #108 ....$200.00–225.00

Vase 12½", heavy crystals, #902 ....$450.00–500.00

Triple Cornucopia, 8" x 12½", heavy crystals, #111 ....$300.00–350.00

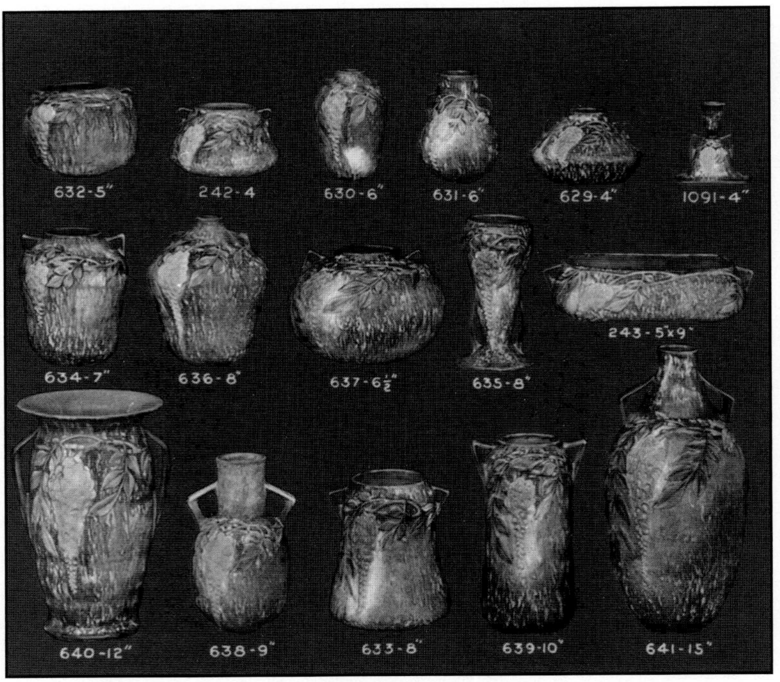

Wisteria

Plate 145

Wisteria

If marked: Foil sticker.

Plate 145
- Vase, 10", #682
  - Tan $750.00–850.00
  - Blue $1,500.00–1,750.00
- Hanging Basket, 7½", #351
  - Tan $500.00–600.00
  - Blue $900.00–1,000.00

Plate 146
- Vase, 8½", #635
  - Tan $550.00–600.00
  - Blue $800.00–900.00
- Vase, 8½", #680
  - Tan $550.00–600.00
  - Blue $900.00–1,000.00
- Bowl Vase, 5", #632
  - Tan $275.00–300.00
  - Blue $450.00–500.00

Plate 146

Plate 147

Jonquil

If marked: Foil or paper sticker.

Plate 147

Row 1:

- Bowl, 3", #523 .... $150.00–200.00
- Candlestick, 4", #1082, pair $400.00–450.00
- Center Bowl, 3½" x 9", #219 .... $275.00–325.00
- Vase, 4½", #101 .... $250.00–300.00
- Vase, 4", #524 .... $200.00–250.00

Row 2:

- Jardiniere, 4", #621 .... $200.00–250.00
- Vase, 5½", #542 .... $325.00–375.00
- Pot/Frog, 5½" (1-pc.), #94 .... $400.00–450.00
- Vase, 4½", #93 .... $375.00–425.00

Row 3:

- Vase, 7", #541 .... $350.00–400.00
- Vase, 6½", #526 .... $400.00–450.00
- Vase, 6½", #543 .... $400.00–450.00
- Crocus Pot, 7", (1-pc.), #96 .... $800.00–900.00

Row 4:

- Vase, 8", #528 .... $450.00–500.00
- Vase, 9½", #544 .... $550.00–600.00
- Vase, 12", #531 .... $900.00–1,000.00
- Vase, 8", #529 .... $450.00–500.00

Plate 148

"Appeal effectively to the higher aesthetic tastes"—BECKWITH

LONG AGO people of unerring taste discovered that articles of adornment have an immense value in expressing personality in the home.

How true this is of the intriguing *Futura* designs in Roseville Pottery! In the few examples given here you can catch the modernistic beauty of Futura . . . the dashing lines . . . the fearless spirit that Roseville craftsmen have so artfully given them.

In this fascinating pottery, there is an exhilarating variety to select from. There are bowls, vases, candlesticks, wall-pockets, jardinieres, hanging baskets . . . scarcely any two alike . . . delightfully tinted in harmonies of blues, grays, tans, reds and greens.

Certainly Futura lends distinction . . . creates a decorative touch superb and uncommon. And so you will want to see these shapes. They will be shown to you at leading stores, where you can make a choice for yourself, or as unusual gifts.

The abundantly illustrated booklet, "Pottery", is yours for the asking. Write for a copy. You will find it interesting.

THE ROSEVILLE POTTERY CO., *Zanesville, Ohio*

ROSEVILLE POTTERY

Futura

If marked: Foil or paper sticker.

Plate 148

Item	Value
Vase, 10", #434	$3,500.00–4,000.00
Vase, 12½", #394	$900.00–1,000.00

Plate 149

Item	Value
Row 1:	
Vase, 7½", #387 (Gray field)	$800.00–900.00
Vase, 8", #386	$700.00–800.00
Vase, 7", #405	$700.00–800.00
Vase, 6", #380	$400.00–450.00
Pillow Vase, 5" x 6", #81	$300.00–350.00
Row 2:	
Vase, 4" x 6", #85	$350.00–400.00
Vase, 3½", #190	$350.00–400.00
Fan Vase, 6", #82	$450.00–500.00
Vase, 4", #189	$450.00–500.00
Row 3:	
Window Box, 5" x 15½", #376	$1,750.00–2,000.00
Candlestick, 4", #1072, pair	$900.00–1,000.00
Jardiniere, 6", #616	$375.00–425.00
Row 4:	
Vase, 6½", #421	$350.00–375.00
Vase, 5", #197	$750.00–800.00
Vase, 10", #392	$800.00–900.00
Vase, 8½", #406	$1,750.00–2,000.00
Vase, 7", #382	$325.00–375.00

Plate 149

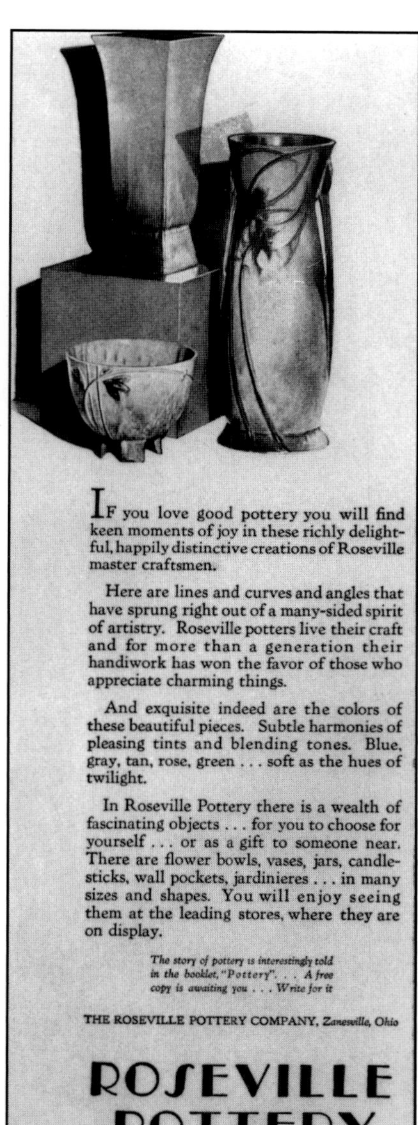
IF you love good pottery you will find keen moments of joy in these richly delightful, happily distinctive creations of Roseville master craftsmen.
Here are lines and curves and angles that have sprung right out of a many-sided spirit of artistry. Roseville potters live their craft and for more than a generation their handiwork has won the favor of those who appreciate charming things.
And exquisite indeed are the colors of these beautiful pieces. Subtle harmonies of pleasing tints and blending tones. Blue, gray, tan, rose, green . . . soft as the hues of twilight.
In Roseville Pottery there is a wealth of fascinating objects . . . for you to choose for yourself . . . or as a gift to someone near. There are flower bowls, vases, jars, candlesticks, wall pockets, jardinieres . . . in many sizes and shapes. You will enjoy seeing them at the leading stores, where they are on display.
The story of pottery is interestingly told in the booklet, "Pottery". . . A free copy is awaiting you . . . Write for it
THE ROSEVILLE POTTERY COMPANY, Zanesville, Ohio
ROSEVILLE POTTERY

Futura

If marked: Foil or paper sticker.

Plate 150

Row 1:
- Vase, 5", #421 .... $350.00–375.00
- Center Bowl, 2½" x 10½", #195 .... $900.00–1,000.00
  - matching frog $400.00–500.00
- Vase, 6", #423 .... $375.00–425.00

Row 2:
- Center Bowl, 3½", #187 .... $375.00–425.00
  - matching frog $75.00–100.00
- Center Bowl, 3½", #196 .... $450.00–500.00
  - matching frog $75.00–100.00
- Center Bowl, 4", #188 .... $500.00–550.00
  - matching frog $75.00–100.00

Row 3:
- Vase, 8", #384 .... $450.00–500.00
- Vase, 7½", #400 .... $700.00–800.00
- Vase, 9½", #412 .... $10,000.00–12,000.00
- Vase, 9", #409 .... $900.00–1,000.00

Row 4:
- Vase, 9", #429 .... $900.00–1,100.00
- Vase, 10", #432 .... $700.00–800.00
- Vase, 15½", #438 .... $1,200.00–1,400.00
- Vase, 10", #431 .... $1,000.00–1,200.00
- Vase, 8", #402 .... $650.00–750.00

Plate 151

Row 1:
- Vase, 8", #383 .... $500.00–600.00
- Vase, 7", #403 .... $1,500.00–1,750.00
- Vase, 9", #388 .... $650.00–750.00

Row 2:
- Vase, 9", #430 .... $1,250.00–1,500.00
- Vase, 10", #435 .... $1,800.00–2,000.00
- Vase, 8", #427 .... $800.00–900.00

Plate 150

Plate 151

"Ever-varying features of the
enrapturing spirit of beauty."—ANON.
THIS delightful new pottery by Roseville—Futura—brings into your home the charm and the exhilarating tang of the modern. There are bowls, vases and other pieces in exquisite shapes and soft colors. They make wonderfully interesting gifts. Leading stores have them.
Send for a copy of the handsomely illustrated free booklet, "Pottery"
THE ROSEVILLE POTTERY CO., ZANESVILLE, OHIO.
ROSEVILLE
POTTERY

Plate 152

Plate 153

Laurel

If marked: Foil sticker.

Plate 152

Item	Color	Price	Color	Price	Color	Price
Vase, 10", #676	Gold	$400.00–450.00	Russet	$500.00–550.00	Green	$650.00–700.00
Vase, 9½", #674	Gold	$350.00–400.00	Russet	$450.00–550.00	Green	$600.00–650.00
Vase, 6½", #250	Gold	$275.00–300.00	Russet	$375.00–400.00	Green	$500.00–550.00
Bowl, 3½", #252	Gold	$225.00–250.00	Russet	$250.00–300.00	Green	$300.00–350.00

Montacello

If marked: Paper sticker.

Plate 153

Item	Color	Price	Color	Price
Basket, 6", #332	Turquoise	$800.00–900.00	Tan	$600.00–700.00
Vase, 5", #557	Turquoise	$350.00–400.00	Tan	$275.00–325.00
Vase, 8", #563	Turquoise	$575.00–625.00	Tan	$425.00–475.00
Vase, 10", #565	Turquoise	$900.00–1,000.00	Tan	$750.00–800.00

Tourmaline

If marked: Foil sticker.

Plate 154

Row 1:
- Vase, 5½", #A-517 ....$100.00–125.00
- Candlesticks, 5", pair, #1089 ....$175.00–200.00
- Pillow Vase, 6", #A-65 ....$100.00–125.00
- Vase, 6", #A-517 ....$100.00–125.00

Row 2:
- Vase, 4½", #A-200 ....$90.00–100.00
- Vase, 7", #A-472 ....$125.00–150.00
- Vase, 6", #611 ....$125.00–150.00
- Bowl, 8", #A-152 ....$75.00–100.00

Row 3:
- Cornucopia, 7" $75.00–100.00
- Vase, 7", #A-308 ....$75.00–100.00
- Vase, 8", #A-332 ....$150.00–175.00
- Vase, 7½", #612...................$100.00–125.00
- Vase, 5½", #238.....................$80.00–100.00

Row 4:
- Vase, 8", #A-425 ....$100.00–125.00
- Vase, 8", #A-673 ....$150.00–175.00
- Vase, 10", #616 ....$250.00–275.00
- Vase, 8" $150.00–175.00
- Vase, 8", #614 ....$150.00–175.00

Plate 154

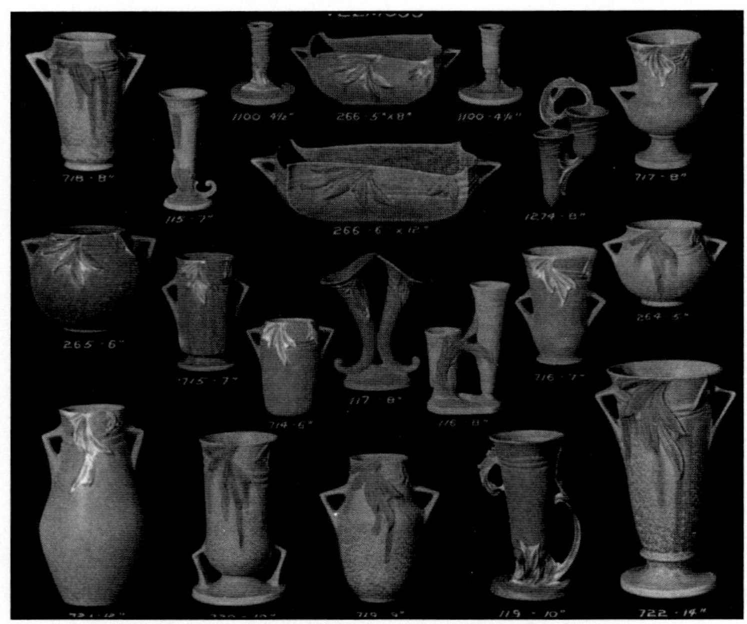

Velmoss II

Plate 155

Plate 156

Velmoss

If marked: Foil sticker.

Plate 155

Item	Green	Blue	Red	Tan (rare)
Vase, 14½", #722	$600.00–650.00	$700.00–750.00	$800.00–850.00	$900.00–950.00
Bowl, 3" x 11", #266	$175.00–225.00	$225.00–275.00	$275.00–325.00	$325.00–375.00

Plate 156

Item	Green	Blue	Red	Tan (rare)
Vase, 8", #718	$225.00–275.00	$300.00–350.00	$350.00–400.00	$400.00–450.00
Vase, 12½", #721	$400.00–450.00	$500.00–550.00	$550.00–600.00	$600.00–650.00
Vase, 9½", #719	$275.00–325.00	$350.00–400.00	$400.00–450.00	$450.00–500.00

Plate 157

Sunflower

If marked: Paper sticker.

Plate 157

Row 1:

Bowl, 4" $450.00–500.00
Vase, 5" $450.00–500.00
Vase, 5" $450.00–500.00
Bowl, 4", #208 ....$500.00–550.00

Row 2:

Candlesticks, 4", pair $800.00–900.00
Center Bowl, 3" x 12½" $800.00–900.00

Row 3:

Vase, 5", #486 ....$700.00–800.00
Window Box, 3½" x 11" $1,300.00–1,500.00
Vase, 6" $550.00–650.00

Row 4:

Vase, 7", #489 ....$1,300.00–1,500.00
Vase, 10", #494 ....$1,500.00–1,750.00
Jardiniere, 6", #619 ....$900.00–1,000.00

Pine Cone

Marks: Roseville impressed or in relief; paper sticker; Pine Cone impressed.

Plate 158

Row 1:

Item	Green	Brown	Blue
Planter, 5", #124	$150.00–175.00	$200.00–250.00	$250.00–300.00
Centerpiece/candle holder, 6", #324	$450.00–550.00	$650.00–750.00	$900.00–1,000.00
Bowl, 4½", #320–5	$150.00–175.00	$200.00–250.00	$250.00–300.00

Row 2:

Item	Green	Brown	Blue
Bowl, 4½", #457–7	$150.00–175.00	$250.00–300.00	$300.00–350.00
Window Box, 3½" x 15½", #431–15	$175.00–200.00	$350.00–400.00	$575.00–650.00
Ashtray, 4½", #499	$100.00–125.00	$175.00–200.00	$200.00–225.00

Plate 158

Row 3:

Candlestick, 2½", #112–3, pair
- Green $100.00–125.00
- Brown $150.00–175.00
- Blue $175.00–200.00

Mug, 4", #960–4
- Green $175.00–200.00
- Brown $350.00–400.00
- Blue $400.00–450.00

Pitcher, 9½", #708–9
- Green $400.00–450.00
- Brown $600.00–700.00
- Blue $900.00–1,000.00

Tumbler, 5", #414
- Green $125.00–150.00
- Brown $250.00–300.00
- Blue $375.00–425.00

Candlestick, 5", #1099–4½, pair
- Green $125.00–150.00
- Brown $225.00–275.00
- Blue $275.00–350.00

Row 4:

Vase, 10½", #747–10
- Green $250.00–275.00
- Brown $500.00–550.00
- Blue $750.00–850.00

Vase, 14½", #850–14
- Green $400.00–450.00
- Brown $800.00–900.00
- Blue $1,250.00–1,500.00

Pitcher, 10½", #485–10
- Green $350.00–400.00
- Brown $600.00–700.00
- Blue $850.00–950.00

Pine Cone

Marks: Roseville impressed or in relief; paper sticker; Pine Cone impressed.

Plate 159

Row 1:

Bud Vase, 7½", #479–7, in Apple Blossom Pink,
(this is the only piece ever reported in this color) $2,000.00–2,500.00

Pillow Vase, 8", #845–8 ....Green...............$300.00–325.00 Brown..............$500.00–550.00 Blue......................$750.00–850.00

Boat Dish, 9", #427–2...................Green...............$200.00–250.00 Brown..............$400.00–450.00 Blue......................$600.00–700.00

Row 2:

Vase, 7", #907–7
Green....................................$125.00–150.00
Brown...................................$275.00–325.00
Blue......................................$375.00–450.00

Center Bowl, 11"
Green......................................$150.00–175.00
Brown.....................................$275.00–325.00
Blue..$400.00–450.00

Vase, 7", #121–7
Green......................................$125.00–150.00
Brown.....................................$275.00–325.00
Blue..$400.00–450.00

Vase, 8½", #490–8
Green......................................$150.00–175.00
Brown.....................................$400.00–450.00
Blue..$575.00–650.00

Row 3:

Vase, 7", #745–7
Green....................................$200.00–225.00
Brown...................................$475.00–525.00
Blue......................................$750.00–850.00

Double Tray, 13", #462
Green....................................$200.00–225.00
Brown...................................$475.00–525.00
Blue......................................$750.00–850.00

Vase, 5", #261
Green....................................$150.00–175.00
Brown...................................$275.00–325.00
Blue......................................$450.00–500.00

Row 4:

Vase, 8", #706
Green....................................$200.00–225.00
Brown...................................$425.00–475.00
Blue......................................$650.00–750.00

Basket, 11", #353–11
Green....................................$250.00–275.00
Brown...................................$500.00–550.00
Blue...................................$950.00–1,100.00

Vase, 8", #908–8
Green....................................$200.00–225.00
Brown...................................$400.00–450.00
Blue......................................$650.00–750.00

Plate 159

Artcraft

If marked: Foil sticker.

Plate 160

Item	Color	Price
Jardiniere, 4"	red	$150.00–175.00
	tan	$200.00–250.00
	blue/green	$250.00–300.00

Plate 160

This label revealed the name of the elegant Art Deco Artcraft line. You'll see two sets of jardinieres and pedestals from this line in the color plates on page 201. (Only jardinieres and pedestals were made.) Besides the red shown here, Artcraft was made in a beautiful blue-green similar to the Earlam glaze and a warm mottled tan that appears to have been made from Futura glaze formulas. This red glaze is as incongrous with these soft glazes as Red Topeo seems to that line; but until an answer is found regarding the mysterious "red line," Red Topeo... Red Artcraft seems to be the most logical terms of reference.

Topeo

If marked: Foil sticker.

Plate 161

Row 1:				
Center Bowl, 3" x 11½"	Red	$100.00–125.00	Blue	$200.00–250.00
Row 2:				
Vase, 7"	Red	$150.00–200.00	Blue	$350.00–400.00
Center Bowl, 4" x 13"	Red	$250.00–300.00	Blue	$400.00–450.00
Vase, 6"	Red	$250.00–300.00	Blue	$450.00–500.00
Row 3:				
Vase, 14"	Red	$900.00–1,000.00	Blue	$1,500.00–2,000.00
Vase, 9"	Red	$275.00–325.00	Blue	$500.00–550.00
Vase, 15"	Red	$1,500.00–2,00.00	Blue	$3,000.00–3,500.00

Plate 162

Center Bowl, 13"	Red	$250.00–300.00	Blue	$400.00–450.00
Double Candlestick, 5", pair	Red	$300.00–350.00	Blue	$550.00–600.00

Plate 163

Vase, 9"	Red	$325.00–375.00	Blue	$600.00–700.00

In trial color, yellow, as shown (indicated by a series of numbers)..........$1,250.00–1,500.00

It has always been a question in the minds of Roseville collectors — were those Topeo shapes glazed in red truly Topeo or were they actually from a separate line? We still don't have the answer.

Plate 161

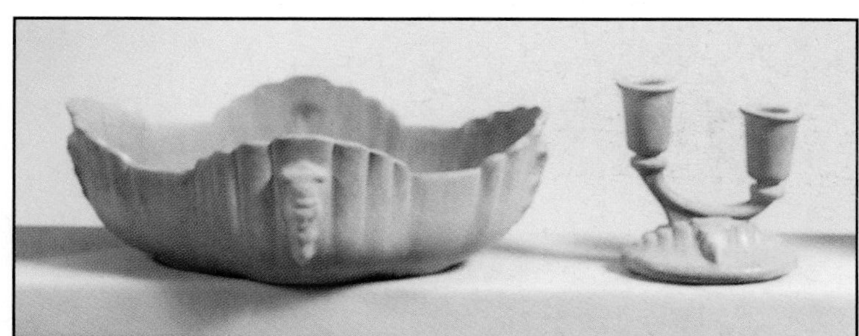

Plate 162

Plate 163

Plate 164

Moss

Mark: Roseville impressed.

Plate 164

Item	Colors	Value	Colors	Value
Bowl Vase, 6", #290	Pink/Green or Orange/Green	$350.00–400.00	Blue	$300.00–350.00
Pillow Vase, 8", #781	Pink/Green or Orange/Green	$350.00–400.00	Blue	$300.00–350.00
Candlestick, 2", #1109, pair	Pink/Green or Orange/Green	$200.00–225.00	Blue	$150.00–175.00
Triple Candlestick, 7", #1108, pair	Pink/Green or Orange/Green	$800.00–900.00	Blue	$600.00 – 700.00

Luffa*

If marked: Foil sticker.

Plate 165

Row 1:

- Vase, 8", #689 .... $650.00–750.00
- Jardiniere, 7", #631 .... $350.00–400.00
- Vase, 6", #683 .... $350.00–400.00
- Candlestick, 5", #1097, pair $500.00–600.00

Row 2:

- Lamp, 9½", blue/green glaze $1,000.00–1,200.00
- Vase, 15½" $1,750.00–2,000.00
- Lamp, 9½", blue/rose glaze $1,000.00–1,200.00

* Unless other colors are specifically indicated, values are given for green and brown examples.

Plate 165

Clemana

Mark: Roseville impressed.

Plate 166

Row 1:

Item	Blue	Green	Tan
Bowl, 4½" x 6½", #281	$250.00–275.00	$225.00–250.00	$200.00–225.00
Vase, 7½", #112	$450.00–500.00	$350.00–400.00	$300.00–350.00
Flower Frog, 4", #23	$200.00–225.00	$175.00–200.00	$150.00–175.00

Row 2:

Vase, 6½", #749
- Blue $250.00–275.00
- Green $225.00–250.00
- Tan $200.00–225.00

Vase, 6½", #280
- Blue $400.00–450.00
- Green $350.00–400.00
- Tan $300.00–350.00

Vase, 7½", #752
- Blue $300.00–350.00
- Green $250.00–300.00
- Tan $225.00–250.00

Vase, 6½", #750
- Blue $250.00–275.00
- Green $225.00–250.00
- Tan $200.00–225.00

Row 3:

Vase, 8½", #754
- Blue $500.00–550.00
- Green $450.00–500.00
- Tan $400.00–450.00

Vase, 12½", #758
- Blue $600.00–650.00
- Green $550.00–600.00
- Tan $500.00–550.00

Vase, 14", #759
- Blue $700.00–800.00
- Green $600.00–700.00
- Tan $500.00–600.00

Vase, 9½", #756
- Blue $550.00–600.00
- Green $500.00–550.00
- Tan $450.00–550.00

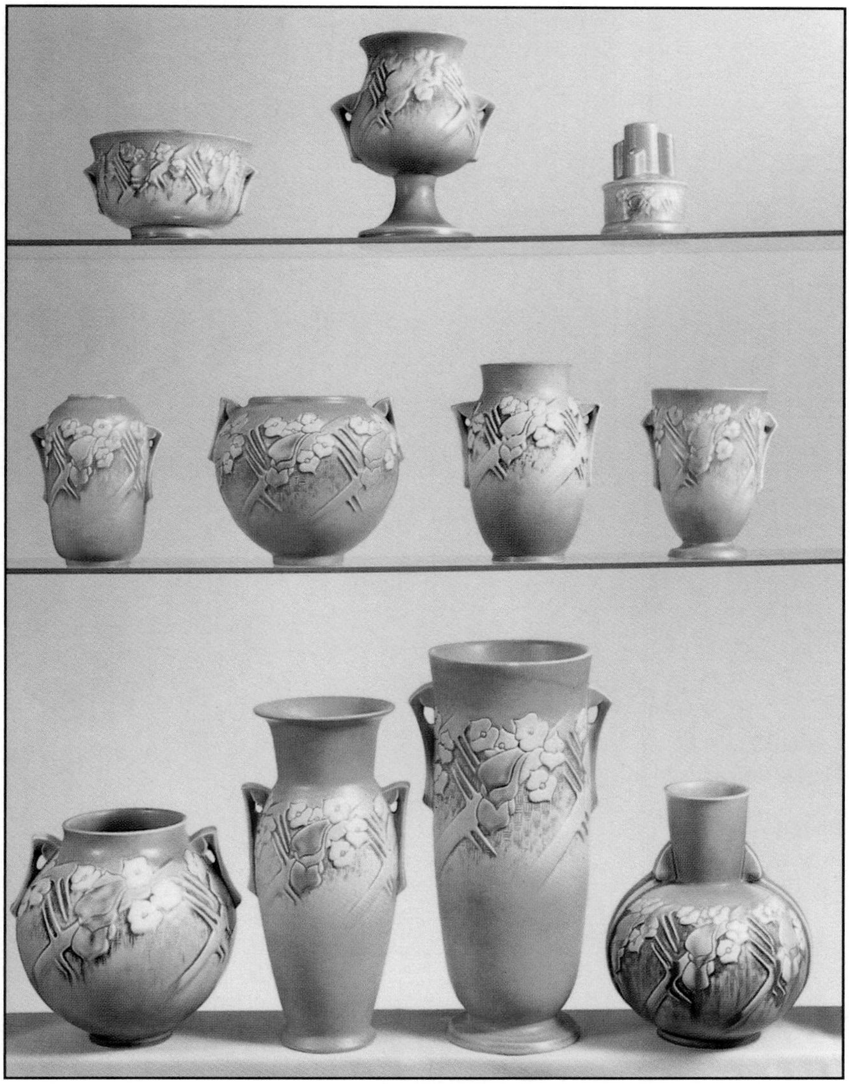

Plate 166

Plate 167

Orian

Marks: Foil sticker; Roseville impressed.

Plate 167

Row 1:

Vase, 6", #733

Tan	$200.00–225.00
Turquoise	$225.00–250.00
Yellow	$250.00–275.00
Red	$275.00–300.00

Vase, 9", #738

Tan	$325.00–375.00
Turquoise	$375.00–400.00
Yellow	$400.00–425.00
Red	$425.00–450.00

Candle Holder, 4½", #1108, pair

Tan	$300.00–350.00
Turquoise	$325.00–375.00
Yellow	$350.00–400.00
Red	$375.00–425.00

Row 2:

Vase, 7", #734

Tan	$225.00–250.00
Turquoise	$250.00–275.00
Yellow	$275.00–300.00
Red	$300.00–325.00

Center Bowl, 5" x 12", #275

Tan	$300.00–325.00
Turquoise	$325.00–350.00
Yellow	$350.00–375.00
Red	$375.00–400.00

Vase, 6½", #733

Tan	$200.00–225.00
Turquoise	$225.00–250.00
Yellow	$250.00–275.00
Red	$275.00–300.00

Plate 168

Orian

Marks: Foil sticker; Roseville impressed.

Plate 168

Vase, 12½", #742
- Tan $450.00–500.00
- Turquoise $475.00–525.00
- Yellow $525.00–575.00
- Red $575.00–650.00

Vase, 10½", #740
- Tan $325.00–375.00
- Turquoise $375.00–400.00
- Yellow $400.00–425.00
- Red $425.00–450.00

Vase, 7½", #737
- Tan $425.00–475.00
- Turquoise $475.00–500.00
- Yellow $500.00–525.00
- Red $525.00–550.00

Compote, 4½" x 10½", #272
- Tan $225.00–250.00
- Turquoise $250.00–275.00
- Yellow $275.00–300.00
- Red $300.00–325.00

Plate 169

Falline

If marked: Foil sticker.

Plate 169

Row 1:

Vase, 6", #650
- Blue....................$1,300.00–1,500.00
- Tan....................$600.00–700.00

Vase, 6", #642
- Blue....................$750.00–850.00
- Tan....................$450.00–500.00

Candle Holder, 4", #1092, pair
- Blue....................$800.00–900.00
- Tan....................$600.00–700.00

Center Bowl, 11", #244
- Blue....................$450.00–500.00
- Tan....................$300.00–350.00

Row 2:

Vase, 8", #646
- Blue....................$1,000.00–1,250.00
- Tan....................$600.00–700.00

Vase, 12½", #653
- Blue....................$2,000.00–2,250.00
- Tan....................$1,000.00–1,100.00

Vase, 9", #652
- Blue....................$1,500.00–1,750.00
- Tan....................$800.00–900.00

Vase, 7½", #647
- Blue....................$800.00–900.00
- Tan....................$500.00–600.00

Plate 170

Ferella

If marked: Paper sticker.

Plate 170

Row 1:

Vase, 6", #505

Tan $600.00–700.00

Red $800.00–900.00

*Lamp Base, 10½"

In any color $1,000.00–1,250.00

Vase, 8", #508

Tan $800.00–900.00

Red $1,000.00–1,200.00

Row 2:

Vase, 6", #499

Tan $400.00–450.00

Red $650.00–750.00

Row 2 (continued):

Candlesticks, 4½", #1078, pair

Tan $500.00–600.00

Red $800.00–900.00

Bowl/Frog, 5", #211

Tan $600.00–700.00

Red $900.00–1,000.00

Vase, 4", #498

Tan $300.00–350.00

Red $500.00–550.00

*Though the lamp base has characteristics very similar to Ferella, it does not actually belong in this lineup. Roseville made many styles of these bases which they sold to lamp companies who added their own hardware. Examples of the Flexo Company's lamps are shown on pages 210 and 211.

Plate 171

Thorn Apple

Mark: Roseville impressed.

Plate 171

Row 1:

- Vase, 8½", #816–8 ....$250.00–300.00
- Double Bud Vase, 5½", #1119....................................$175.00–225.00
- Hanging Basket, 7" dia...........................$300.00–350.00
- Triple Bud Vase, 6", #1120....................$200.00–250.00

Row 2:

- Bowl Vase, 6½", #305–6........................$200.00–250.00
- Vase, 10½", #822–10 ....$300.00–350.00
- Vase, 9½", #820–9 ....$275.00–325.00

Earlam

If marked: Paper sticker.

Plate 172

Row 1:

- Vase, 4", #515...................................$325.00–350.00
- Vase, 6", #518...................................$450.00–500.00
- Candlestick, 4", #1080, pair $500.00–600.00

Row 2:

- Bowl, 3" x 11½", #218 ....$400.00–450.00
- Vase, 9", #522...................................$650.00–750.00
- Planter, 5½" x 10½", #89 ....$400.00–450.00

Plate 172

Plate 173

Ixia

If marked: Roseville impressed; foil sticker.

Plate 173

Row 1:

Hanging Basket, 7"................................$200.00–250.00

Double Candlestick,
3", #1127 ....$125.00–150.00

Center Bowl,
3½" x 10½", #330–7 ....$125.00–150.00

Candle Holder/Bud Vase,
5", #1128, each................................$150.00–175.00

Row 2:

Vase, 8½", #857–8 ....$150.00–175.00

Vase, 8½", #858–8 ....$175.00–200.00

Vase, 10½", #862–10 ....$225.00–275.00

Vase, 8½", #856–8 ....$175.00–200.00

Windsor

If marked: Foil and paper stickers.

Plate 174

Row 1:

Center Bowl, 3½" x 10½"
Blue..........................$450.00–550.00
Rust..........................$350.00–400.00

Basket, 4½", #330
Blue..........................$800.00–900.00
Rust..........................$600.00–700.00

Center Bowl, 3" x 10"
Blue..........................$400.00–450.00
Rust..........................$300.00–350.00

Row 2:

Vase, 6", #546
Blue..........................$400.00–450.00
Rust..........................$300.00–350.00

Vase, 7", #582
Blue....................$1,500.00–1,750.00
Rust....................$1,000.00–1,250.00

Factory Lamp base 7", #551
Blue.......................$900.00–1,000.00
Rust..........................$700.00–800.00

Plate 174

Moderne

Plate 175

Moderne

Marks: Roseville impressed or foil sticker.

Plate 175

Row 1:

- Triple Candle Holder, 6", #1112 ....$250.00–275.00
- Vase, 6½, #299....................................$200.00–225.00
- Vase, 6½", #787 ....$150.00–175.00

Row 2:

- Compote, 6", #297–6 ....$225.00–250.00
- Vase, 8½", #796–8 ....$225.00–250.00
- Vase, 6", #789–6.................................$200.00–225.00
- Compote, 5", #295 ....$225.00–250.00

Poppy

Mark: Roseville impressed.

Plate 176

Row 1:

Item	Color	Price	Color	Price
Vase, 6$\frac{1}{2}$", #335–6	Pink*	$350.00–400.00	Gray/Green	$250.00–300.00
Vase, 5", #642–4	Pink*	$150.00–175.00	Gray/Green	$125.00–150.00
Bowl, 12", #336–10	Pink*	$225.00–275.00	Gray/Green	$175.00–225.00

Row 2:

Bowl, 3$\frac{1}{2}$", #642–3
- Pink* $100.00–125.00
- Gray/Green $80.00–100.00

Vase, 6", #866–6
- Pink* $125.00–150.00
- Gray/Green $95.00–120.00

Vase, 7$\frac{1}{2}$", #368–7
- Pink* $150.00–175.00
- Gray/Green $125.00–150.00

Vase, 7$\frac{1}{2}$", #869–7
- Pink* $150.00–175.00
- Gray/Green $125.00–150.00

Vase, 8", #870–8
- Pink* $225.00–275.00
- Gray/Green $150.00–175.00

Row 3:

Vase, 9", #872–9
- Pink* $350.00–400.00
- Gray/Green $225.00–275.00

Ewer, 18$\frac{1}{2}$", #880–18
- Pink* $700.00–800.00
- Gray/Green $550.00–650.00

Basket, 12$\frac{1}{2}$", #348–12
- Pink* $500.00–550.00
- Gray/Green $375.00–425.00

Vase, 8", #871–8
- Pink* $300.00–350.00
- Gray/Green $200.00–250.00

* Add 50% for tan.

Plate 176

Primrose

Plate 177

Primrose

Mark: Roseville impressed.

Plate 177

Vase, 6½", #761–6

- Tan $125.00–150.00
- Blue or Pink $150.00–175.00

Vase, 7", #760–6

- Tan $125.00–150.00
- Blue or Pink $150.00–175.00

Primrose

Baneda

If marked: Foil sticker.

Plate 178

Row 1:

Item	Green	Pink
Center Bowl, 3½" x 10", #233	$600.00–700.00	$375.00–425.00
Vase, 4½", #603	$625.00–675.00	$400.00–450.00
Center Bowl, 3" x 11", #234	$700.00–800.00	$475.00–550.00

Row 2:

Item	Green	Pink
Vase, 5", #235	$750.00–825.00	$500.00–550.00
Candle Holder, 5½", #1087, pair	$750.00–825.00	$500.00–550.00
Vase, 7", #606	$750.00–825.00	$550.00–600.00
Vase, 6", #602	$650.00–700.00	$375.00–400.00
Vase, 4", #587	$475.00–525.00	$300.00–350.00

Row 3:

Item	Green	Pink
Vase, 7", #592	$725.00–800.00	$550.00–600.00
Vase, 7", #610	$725.00–800.00	$550.00–600.00
Vase, 9", #594	$1,000.00–1,100.00	$750.00–800.00
Vase, 8", #595	$1,200.00–1,400.00	$800.00–900.00

Row 4:

Item	Green	Pink
Vase, 10", #597	$1,800.00–2,000.00	$1,200.00–1,400.00
Vase, 12", #598	$1,800.00–2,000.00	$1,300.00–1,500.00
Vase, 12", #599	$2,500.00–2,750.00	$1,500.00–1,750.00
Vase, 9", #596	$1,500.00–1,750.00	$1,000.00–1,250.00

Plate 178

Teasel

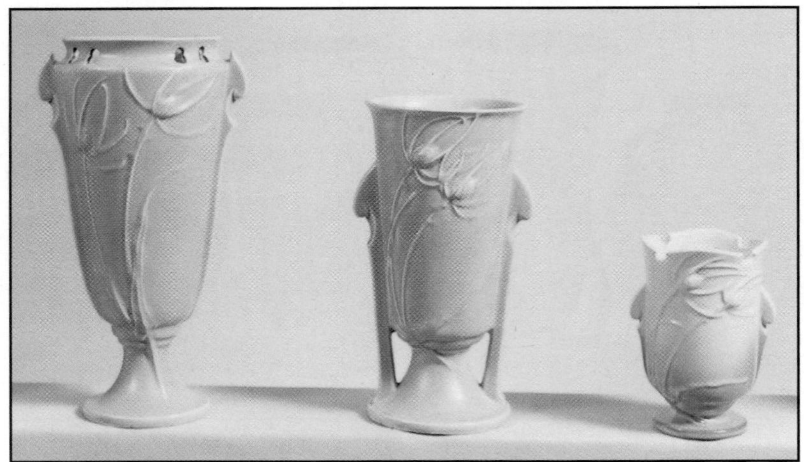

Plate 179

Teasel

Mark: Roseville impressed.

Plate 179

Vase, 12", #888–12
- Dark Blue or Rust $300.00–350.00
- Light Blue or Tan $275.00–325.00

Vase, 10", #887–10
- Dark Blue or Rust $275.00–325.00
- Light Blue or Tan $225.00–275.00

Vase, 6", #881–6
- Dark Blue or Rust $150.00–175.00
- Light Blue or Tan $125.00–150.00

Plate 180

Blackberry

If marked: Foil sticker.

Plate 180

Row 1:

Vase, 6"..$400.00–450.00
Hanging Basket,
4½" x 6½" $600.00–700.00
Basket...$800.00–900.00

Row 2:

Jardiniere, 7"...................................$500.00–550.00
Jardiniere, 6"...................................$400.00–450.00
Jardiniere, 4"...................................$300.00–350.00

Morning Glory

If marked: Foil sticker.

Plate 181

Row 1:

Candlestick, 5", #1102, pair
Green..$650.00–750.00
Ivory...$400.00–450.00
Center Bowl, 4½" x 11½", #270
Green..$475.00–550.00
Ivory...$350.00–375.00
Vase, 5", #723
Green..$350.00–425.00
Ivory...$275.00–325.00

Row 2:

Basket, 10½", #340
Green...$900.00–1,100.00
Ivory...$500.00–550.00
Vase, 14", #732
Green...$1,500.00–1,750.00
Ivory..$900.00–1,000.00
Pillow Vase, 7", #120
Green..$375.00–425.00
Ivory...$275.00–325.00

Plate 181

Plate 182

Plate 183

Dawn

Dawn

Mark: Roseville impressed.

Plate 182

Vase, 12", #833–12

Pink or Yellow $450.00–500.00

Green....................$350.00–400.00

Bowl, 16", #318–14

Pink or Yellow $250.00–275.00

Green....................$200.00–225.00

Plate 183

Ewer, 16", #834–16

Pink or Yellow $600.00–700.00

Green....................$450.00–500.00

Plate 184

Plate 185

Ivory II

Marks: Roseville impressed or in relief; foil sticker.

Plate 184

Row 1:

Cornucopia, 5½" x 12", #2 ....$75.00–95.00
Jardiniere, 4", #574–4..$40.00–50.00
Vase, 6½", #274–6 ....$75.00–95.00

Row 2:

Vase, 7", ...$75.00–95.00
Candlestick, 5½", #1122–5, pair $75.00–95.00
Ewer, 10½", #941–10 ....$75.00–95.00
Candlestick, 2½", #1114–2, pair $40.00–60.00
Jardiniere, 6"..$50.00–75.00

Plate 185

Hanging Basket, 7"..$75.00–100.00
Dog, 6½" $600.00–700.00
Nude, 9"..$1,750.00–2,000.00

Plate 186

Iris

Marks: Roseville impressed or in relief.

Plate 186

Row 1:

Vase, 6½", #917–6
- Blue $175.00–200.00
- Pink or Tan $150.00–175.00

Basket, 9½", #355–10
- Blue $475.00–550.00
- Pink or Tan $425.00–475.00

Vase, 7½", #920–7
- Blue $200.00–225.00
- Pink or Tan $175.00–200.00

Row 2:

Pillow Vase, 8½", #922–8
- Blue $325.00–375.00
- Pink or Tan $275.00–300.00

Center Bowl, 3" x 10", #361–8
- Blue $200.00–225.00
- Pink or Tan $175.00–200.00

Vase, 6½", #358–6
- Blue $325.00–375.00
- Pink or Tan $275.00–300.00

Row 3:

Vase, 3½", #647–3
- Blue $125.00–150.00
- Pink or Tan $100.00–125.00

Center Bowl, 3½" x 12½", #362–10
- Blue $225.00–250.00
- Pink or Tan $200.00–225.00

Vase, 5", #915–5
- Blue $125.00–150.00
- Pink or Tan $100.00–125.00

Row 4:

Vase, 8", #923–8
- Blue $375.00–425.00
- Pink or Tan $300.00–350.00

Vase, 12½", #928–12
- Blue $550.00–650.00
- Pink or Tan $425.00–475.00

Vase, 10", #924–9
- Blue $450.00–475.00
- Pink or Tan $350.00–400.00

Woman's Home Companion, July 1940

Plate 187

Bleeding Heart

Mark: Roseville in relief.

Plate 187

Row 1:

Hanging Basket, 8" diameter, #362
- Blue $325.00–375.00
- Pink or Green $275.00–325.00

Bowl Vase, 3½", #651–3
- Blue $125.00–150.00
- Pink or Green $100.00–125.00

Vase, 8", #969–8
- Blue $250.00–300.00
- Pink or Green $200.00–250.00

Bowl Vase, 4", #377–4
- Blue $125.00–150.00
- Pink or Green $100.00–125.00

Vase, 8½", #968–9
- Blue $250.00–300.00
- Pink or Green $200.00–250.00

Vase, 6½", #964–6
- Blue $175.00–200.00
- Pink or Green $125.00–150.00

Row 2:

Candlesticks, 5", #1139–4½, pair
- Blue $225.00–275.00
- Pink or Green $200.00–250.00

Center Bowl, 17", #384–14, with Frog, #40
- Blue $250.00–300.00
- Pink or Green $175.00–225.00

Row 3:

Basket, 9½", #360–10
- Blue $350.00–400.00
- Pink or Green $275.00–325.00

Vase, 15", #976–15
- Blue $700.00–800.00
- Pink or Green $650.00–750.00

Plate, 10½", #381–10
- Blue $200.00–225.00
- Pink or Green $150.00–175.00

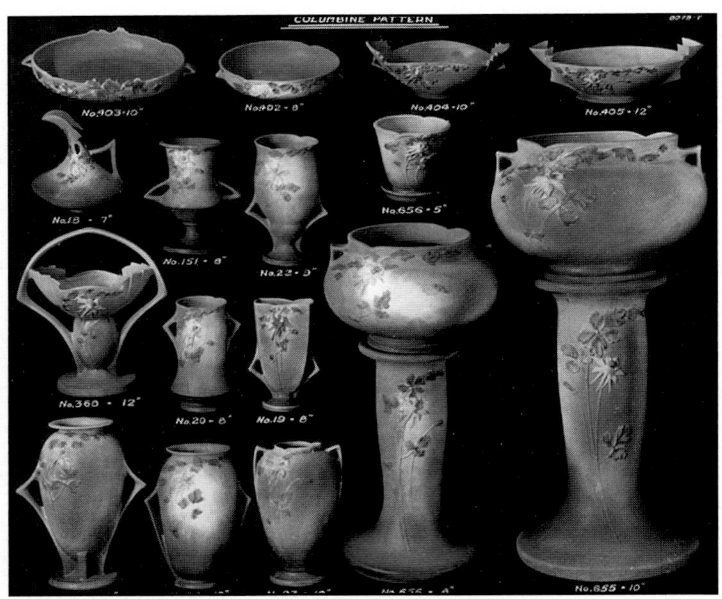

Columbine

Columbine

Mark: Roseville in relief.

Plate 188
- Row 1:
  - Vase, 7½", #17–7
    - Pink $225.00–275.00
    - Blue or Tan $175.00–225.00
  - Hanging Basket, 8½"
    - Pink $375.00–425.00
    - Blue or Tan $325.00–375.00
  - Vase, 8", #151–8
    - Pink $275.00–325.00
    - Blue or Tan $225.00–275.00
- Row 2:
  - Bookend Planter, 5", #8, pair
    - Pink $450.00–550.00
    - Blue or Tan $350.00–400.00
  - Candle Holders, 5", #1146–4½, pair
    - Pink $225.00–250.00
    - Blue or Tan $175.00–200.00
  - Cornucopia, 5½", #149–6
    - Pink $175.00–200.00
    - Blue or Tan $150.00–175.00

Plate 188

Fuchsia

Marks: Roseville impressed or in relief.

Plate 189

Row 1:

Vase, 6" #893–6
- Blue...$250.00–300.00
- Green...$200.00–225.00
- Brown/Tan...$175.00–200.00

Vase, 6", #891–6
- Blue...$250.00–300.00
- Green...$200.00–225.00
- Brown/Tan...$175.00–200.00

Vase, 6", #892–6
- Blue...$250.00–300.00
- Green...$200.00–225.00
- Brown/Tan...$175.00–200.00

Row 2:

Candlesticks, 2", #1132, pair
- Blue...$175.00–200.00
- Green...$150.00–175.00
- Brown/Tan...$125.00–150.00

Center Bowl, 3½" x 12½", #351–10
- Blue...$300.00–350.00
- Green...$225.00–275.00
- Brown/Tan...$200.00–225.00

Row 3:

Candlesticks, 5½", #1133–5, pair
- Blue...$500.00–550.00
- Green...$400.00–450.00
- Brown/Tan...$300.00–350.00

Center Bowl, 4" x 15½", #353–14
- Blue...$375.00–425.00
- Green...$300.00–350.00
- Brown/Tan...$275.00–325.00

Frog, #37
- Blue...$250.00–300.00
- Green...$225.00–250.00
- Brown/Tan...$200.00–225.00

Row 4:

Vase, 8", #897–8
- Blue...$450.00–500.00
- Green...$350.00–400.00
- Brown/Tan...$300.00–350.00

Vase, 8½", #896–8
- Blue...$450.00–500.00
- Green...$350.00–400.00
- Brown/Tan...$300.00–350.00

Vase, 8", #898–8
- Blue...$475.00–525.00
- Green...$375.00–425.00
- Brown/Tan...$325.00–375.00

Plate 189

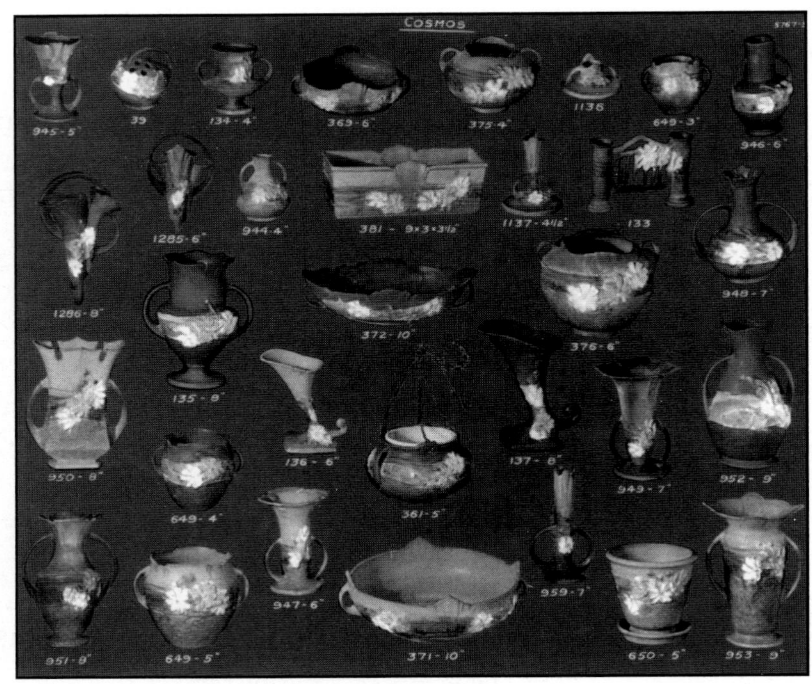

Cosmos

Cosmos

Marks: Roseville impressed or in relief.

Plate 190

Row 1:

Item	Blue	Green	Tan
Hanging Basket, 7", #361	$350.00–400.00	$300.00–350.00	$250.00–300.00
Vase, 8", #950–8	$350.00–400.00	$300.00–350.00	$250.00–300.00
Vase, 5", #945–5	$150.00–175.00	$125.00–150.00	$100.00–125.00
Vase, 4", #375–4	$175.00–225.00	$150.00–175.00	$125.00–150.00
Vase, 6½", #946	$150.00–175.00	$125.00–150.00	$100.00–125.00

Vase, 12½", #956–12
- Blue $450.00–500.00
- Green $400.00–450.00
- Tan $300.00–350.00

Row 2:

Vase, 4", #134–4
- Blue $100.00–125.00
- Green $85.00–95.00
- Tan $75.00–85.00

Center Bowl, 15½", #374–14
- Blue $275.00–325.00
- Green $250.00–300.00
- Tan $200.00–250.00

Flower Frog, 3½", #39
- Blue $150.00–175.00
- Green $125.00–150.00
- Tan $100.00–125.00

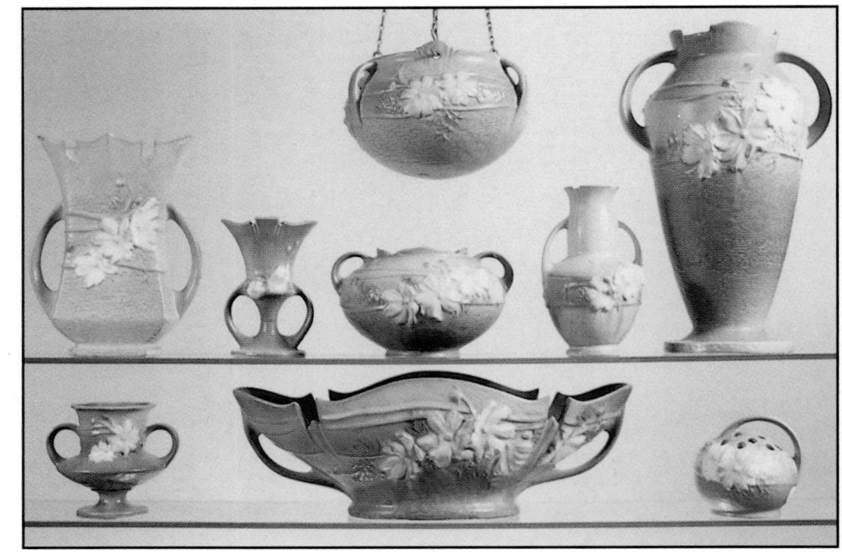

Plate 190

Better Homes and Gardens, late 1940s

Plate 191

White Rose

Mark: Roseville in relief.

Plate 191

Row 1:
- Vase, 4", #978–4 ....$80.00–90.00
- Vase, 5", #980–6 ....$90.00–110.00
- Basket, 7½", #362–8 ....$200.00–250.00
- Vase, 6", #979–6 ....$110.00–135.00
- Candlestick, 4½", #1142–4½", pair $125.00–150.00

Row 2:
- Vase, 7", #388–7 ....$150.00–200.00
- Vase, 8", #984–8 ....$150.00–200.00
- Vase, 8½", #985–8 ....$150.00–200.00

Row 3:
- Double Bud Vase, 4½", #148 ....$85.00–95.00
- Console, Frog, 16½", #393–12, Frog, #41 ....$150.00–200.00
- Double Candle Holder, 4", #1143, pair $200.00–250.00

Row 4:
- Vase 12½", #991–12 ....$250.00–300.00
- Vase, 15½", #992–15 ....$300.00–400.00
- Vase, 9", #987–9 ....$150.00–200.00

Plate 192

Ladies' Home Journal, April 1942

Bittersweet

Mark: Roseville in relief.

Plate 192

Row 1:

- Basket, 8½", #809–8 .... $200.00–250.00
- Vase, 6", #881–6 .... $100.00–125.00
- Bowl Vase, 7", #842–7 .... $200.00–250.00

Row 2:

- Planter, 10½", #828–10 .... $150.00–175.00
- Planter, 11½", #827–8 .... $150.00–175.00
- Cornucopia, 4½", #857–4 .... $100.00–125.00

Row 3:

- Candlesticks, 3", #851–3, pair $150.00–175.00
- Center Bowl, 12½", #829–12 .... $175.00–200.00
- Double Vase, 4", #858 .... $150.00–175.00

Row 4:

- Vase, 7", #874–7 .... $125.00–150.00
- Vase, 10", #885–10 .... $200.00–225.00
- Vase, 15½", #888–16 .... $450.00–500.00
- Vase, 8", #884–8 .... $150.00–175.00

Foxglove

Marks: Roseville in relief or (rarely) impressed.

Plate 193

Row 1:

Tray, 8½", #419
- Green/Pink $200.00–225.00
- Blue $175.00–200.00
- Pink $150.00–175.00

Hanging Basket, 6½", #466
- Green/Pink $350.00–400.00
- Blue $325.00–375.00
- Pink $300.00–350.00

Cornucopia, 6", #166–6
- Green/Pink $200.00–225.00
- Blue $175.00–200.00
- Pink $150.00–175.00

Row 2:

Tray, 15" wide, #424
- Green/Pink $350.00–400.00
- Blue $300.00–350.00
- Pink $250.00–300.00

Flower Frog, 4", #46
- Green/Pink $150.00–175.00
- Blue $125.00–150.00
- Pink $125.00–150.00

Tray, 11", #420 (impressed mark)
- Green/Pink $250.00–300.00
- Blue $225.00–275.00
- Pink $200.00–250.00

Row 3:

Vase, 12½", #52–12
- Green/Pink $450.00–500.00
- Blue $400.00–450.00
- Pink $350.00–400.00

Vase, 14", #53–14
- Green/Pink $500.00–550.00
- Blue $450.00–500.00
- Pink $400.00–450.00

Vase, 10", #51–10
- Green/Pink $350.00–400.00
- Blue $300.00–350.00
- Pink $250.00–300.00

Vase, 8½", #47–8
- Green/Pink $275.00–325.00
- Blue $250.00–300.00
- Pink $225.00–275.00

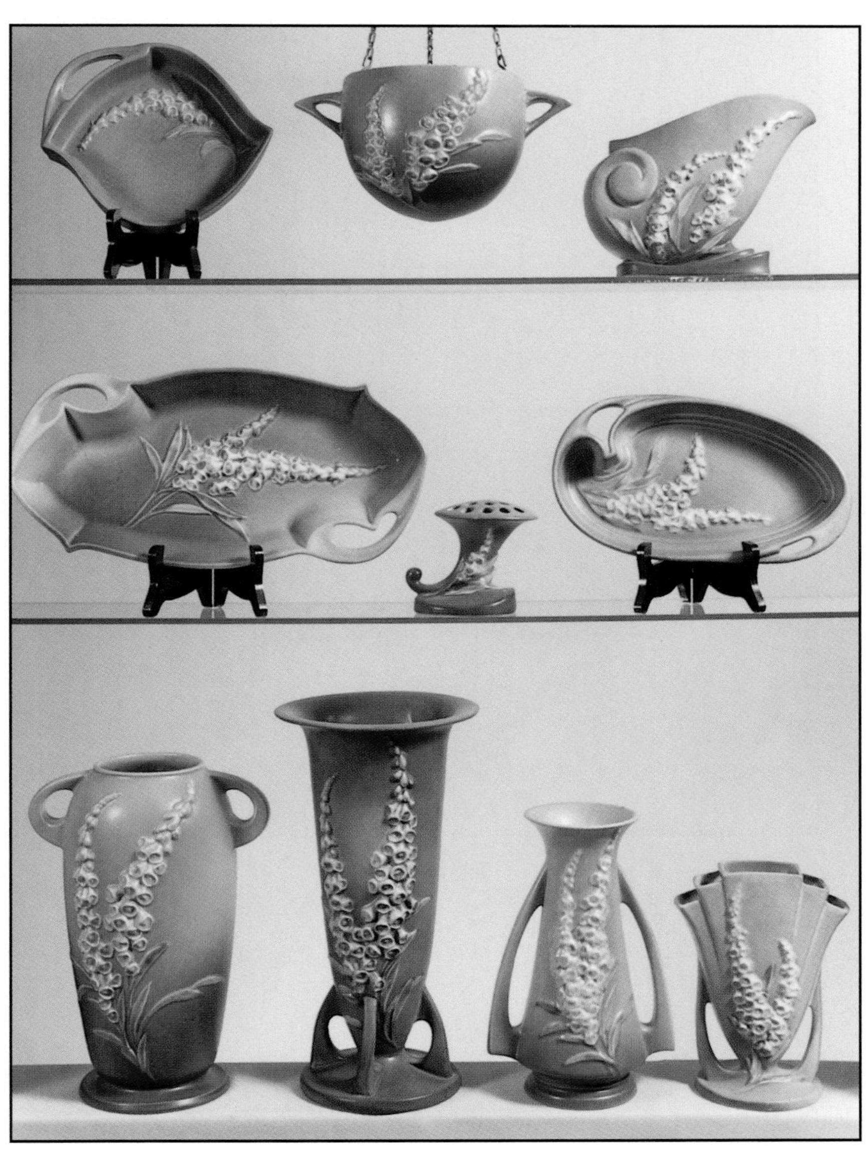

Plate 193

Plate 194

PEONY

DECORATIVE ART POTTERY BY

ROSEVILLE

Beautifully rounded Peony blooms, enhanced by a rich wood-texture finish. 65 graceful new shapes in handpainted Sienna Brown, Coral, Nile Green. At gift shops and department stores.

Send 10c for colorful booklet

ROSEVILLE POTTERY, INC.

Dept. B-102, Zanesville, Ohio

Better Homes and Gardens,
October 1942

Peony

Mark: Roseville in relief.

Plate 194

Row 1:

- Bookend, 5½", #11, pair....................$200.00–250.00
- Conch Shell, 9½", #436....................$110.00–135.00
- Tray, 8"....................$75.00–100.00

Row 2:

- Planter, 10", #387–8....................$85.00–95.00
- Bowl, 11", #430–10....................$100.00–125.00

Row 3:

- Double Candle Holder, 5", #115–3, pair....................$200.00–250.00

Row 3 (continued):

- Mug, 3½", #2–3½....................$100.00–125.00
- Pitcher, 7½", #1326–7½....................$275.00–325.00
- Frog, 4", #47....................$85.00–95.00

Row 4:

- Vase, 8", #169–8....................$125.00–150.00
- Basket, 11", #379–12....................$250.00–275.00
- Vase, 14", #68–14....................$300.00–350.00

Homes Beautiful, July 1943

Plate 195

Magnolia

Mark: Roseville in relief.

Plate 195

Row 1:

- Planter, 8½", #388–6, Brown or Green $85.00–95.00
  - Blue $135.00–145.00
- Planter, 6", #183–6, Brown or Green....................$90.00–110.00
  - Blue $140.00–160.00
- Candlestick, 5", #1157–4½, pair
  - Brown or Green $120.00–150.00
  - Blue $170.00–200.00
- Candlestick, 2½", #1156–2½, pair
  - Brown or Green $100.00–125.00
  - Blue $150.00–175.00

Row 2:

- Ashtray, 7", #28, Brown or Green $100.00–125.00
  - Blue $150.00–175.00
- Center Bowl, 14½", #5–10, Brown or Green....................$125.00–175.00
  - Blue $175.00–225.00
- Cornucopia, 6", #184–6, Brown or Green....................$85.00–95.00
  - Blue $135.00–145.00

Row 3:

- Vase, 6", #180–6, Brown or Green $95.00–110.00
  - Blue $145.00–160.00
- Flower Frog, 5½", #182–5, Brown or Green $95.00–110.00
  - Blue $145.00–160.00
- Conch Shell, 6½", #453–6, Brown or Green $95.00–110.00
  - Blue $145.00–160.00
- Vase, 6", #88–6, Brown or Green $95.00–110.00
  - Blue $145.00–160.00

Row 4:

- Basket, 12", #386–12, Brown or Green....................$275.00–325.00
  - Blue $325.00–375.00
- Ewer, 10", #14–10, Brown or Green $175.00–200.00
  - Blue $225.00–250.00
- Vase, 8", #91–8, Brown or Green $125.00–150.00
  - Blue $175.00–200.00

Plate 196

Water Lily

Mark: Roseville in relief.

Plate 196

Vase, 9", #78–9
- Rose with Green $250.00–300.00
- Blue $225.00–275.00
- Brown $200.00–250.00

Candlesticks, 5", #1155–4½, pair
- Rose with Green $175.00–225.00
- Blue $150.00–200.00
- Brown $125.00–175.00

Hanging Basket, 9", #468, U.S.A.
- Rose with Green $275.00–325.00
- Blue $250.00–300.00
- Brown $225.00–275.00

Frog, 4½", #48
- Rose with Green $125.00–150.00
- Blue $110.00–130.00
- Brown with Green $100.00–110.00

Water Lily

Freesia

Mark: Roseville in relief.

Plate 197

Row 1:

Flowerpot/Saucer, 5½", #670–5
- Green................................$175.00–200.00
- Blue..................................$150.00–175.00
- Tangerine..........................$125.00–150.00

Basket, 7", #390–7
- Green................................$150.00–175.00
- Blue..................................$125.00–150.00
- Tangerine..........................$100.00–125.00

Jardiniere, 4", #669–4
- Green................................$100.00–125.00
- Blue..................................$85.00–95.00
- Tangerine..........................$75.00–85.00

Row 2:

Center Bowl, 8½", #464–6
- Green................................$150.00–175.00
- Blue..................................$125.00–150.00
- Tangerine..........................$100.00–125.00

Bowl, 11", #465–8
- Green................................$175.00–200.00
- Blue..................................$150.00–175.00
- Tangerine..........................$125.00–150.00

Row 3:

Candle Holders, 2", #1160–2, pair
- Green................................$110.00–120.00
- Blue..................................$90.00–100.00
- Tangerine..............................$80.00–90.00

Center Bowl, 16½", #469–14
- Green................................$275.00–325.00
- Blue..................................$225.00–275.00
- Tangerine..........................$200.00–250.00

Row 4:

Vase, 5", #463–5
- Green................................$175.00–200.00
- Blue..................................$150.00–175.00
- Tangerine..........................$125.00–150.00

Vase, 7", #119–7........................Green...............$150.00–175.00 Blue.....................$125.00–150.00 Tangerine $100.00–125.00

Window Box, 10½", #1392–8 ....Green...............$175.00–200.00 Blue.....................$150.00–175.00 Tangerine $125.00–150.00

Row 5:

Vase, 8", #212–8........................Green...............$175.00–200.00 Blue.....................$150.00–175.00 Tangerine $125.00–150.00

Vase, 9½", #123–9 ....Green...............$185.00–210.00 Blue.....................$165.00–185.00 Tangerine $150.00–170.00

Vase, 10½", #125–10 ....Green...............$195.00–225.00 Blue.....................$175.00–195.00 Tangerine $150.00–170.00

Vase, 9", #124–9........................Green...............$185.00–210.00 Blue.....................$165.00–185.00 Tangerine $150.00–170.00

Plate 197

The American Home, July 1945

Plate 198

Rozane Pattern

Mark: Roseville in relief.

Plate 198

Vase, 12", #10–12 .... $350.00–400.00
Bowl, 7½", #8–8; with ornament, 5", #1, set $300.00–350.00
Vase, 8½", #5–8 .... $200.00–225.00

Company booklet featuring Zephyr Lily ewer.

Better Homes and Gardens, October 1946

Zephyr Lily

Mark: Roseville in relief.

Plate 199

Row 1:

Fan Vase, 6½", #205–6
- Blue $175.00–200.00
- Brown $150.00–175.00
- Green $125.00–150.00

Hanging Basket, 7½"
- Blue $350.00–400.00
- Brown $300.00–350.00
- Green $275.00–300.00

Pillow Vase, 7", #206–7
- Blue $225.00–275.00
- Brown $200.00–225.00
- Green $175.00–200.00

Row 2:

Candle Holders, 2", #1162–2, pair
- Blue $150.00–175.00
- Brown $125.00–150.00
- Green $100.00–175.00

Center Bowl, 16½", #479–14
- Blue $250.00–275.00
- Brown $225.00–250.00
- Green $200.00–225.00

Bud Vase, 7½", #201–7
- Blue $175.00–200.00
- Brown $150.00–175.00
- Green $125.00–150.00

Row 3:

Vase, 8½", #133–8
- Blue $175.00–200.00
- Brown $150.00–175.00
- Green $125.00–150.00

Tray, 14½"
- Blue $250.00–275.00
- Brown $225.00–250.00
- Green $200.00–225.00

Cornucopia, 8½", #204–8
- Blue $175.00–200.00
- Brown $150.00–175.00
- Green $125.00–150.00

Plate 199

Row 4:

Vase, 9½", #135–9	Blue $250.00–275.00	Brown....$225.00–250.00	Green $200.00–225.00
Vase, 12", #139–12	Blue $350.00–400.00	Brown....$300.00–350.00	Green $275.00–300.00
Vase, 12½", #140–12	Blue $375.00–425.00	Brown....$325.00–375.00	Green $300.00–325.00
Vase, 8½", #202–8	Blue $250.00–275.00	Brown....$225.00–250.00	Green ....$$200.00–225.00

Plate 200

Clematis

Mark: Roseville in relief.

Plate 200

Item	Color	Price	Color	Price
Row 1:				
Center Bowl, 14", #458–10	Blue	$200.00–250.00	Green or Brown	$175.00–200.00
Candle Holder, 2½", #1158–2, pair	Blue	$110.00–130.00	Green or Brown	$95.00–110.00
Center Bowl, 9", #456–6	Blue	$150.00–175.00	Green or Brown	$125.00–150.00
Row 2:				
Flower Arranger, 5½", #192–5	Blue	$100.00–125.00	Green or Brown	$90.00–110.00
Flowerpot with Saucer, 5½", #668–5	Blue	$175.00–200.00	Green or Brown	$150.00–175.00
Vase, 6", #103–6	Blue	$100.00–125.00	Green or Brown	$90.00–110.00
Flower Frog, 4½", #50	Blue	$95.00–110.00	Green or Brown	$80.00–95.00
Vase, 6½", #102–6	Blue	$110.00–130.00	Green or Brown	$95.00–110.00

The American Home, Feb. 1945

Company brochure and envelope

Snowberry

Mark: Roseville in relief

Plate 201

Row 1:

- Vase, 6", #1RB–6
  - Blue or Pink....................$200.00–225.00
  - Green....................$150.00–175.00
- Pillow Vase, 6½", #1FH–6
  - Blue or Pink....................$150.00–175.00
  - Green....................$100.00–125.00
- Flowerpot, 5½", #1PS–5
  - Blue or Pink....................$225.00–250.00
  - Green....................$200.00–225.00

Row 2:

- Candlesticks, 4½", #1CS–2, pair
  - Blue or Pink....................$175.00–225.00
  - Green....................$150.00–175.00
- Center Bowl, 11", #1BL–8
  - Blue or Pink....................$150.00–175.00
  - Green....................$125.00–150.00

Row 3:

- Vase, 6", #1V–6
  - Blue or Pink....................$90.00–110.00
  - Green....................$70.00–85.00
- Tray, 14", #1BL–12
  - Blue or Pink....................$250.00–275.00
  - Green....................$200.00–225.00
- Vase, 7½", #1V2–7
  - Blue or Pink....................$110.00–130.00
  - Green....................$85.00–100.00

Row 4:

- Vase, 12½", #1V1–12
  - Blue or Pink....................$300.00–350.00
  - Green....................$275.00–300.00
- Ewer, 16", #1TK–15
  - Blue or Pink....................$450.00–500.00
  - Green....................$375.00–425.00
- Basket, 12½", #1BK–12
  - Blue or Pink....................$350.00–375.00
  - Green....................$275.00–325.00
- Vase, 8½", #1UR–8
  - Blue or Pink....................$225.00–250.00
  - Green....................$175.00–200.00

Plate 201

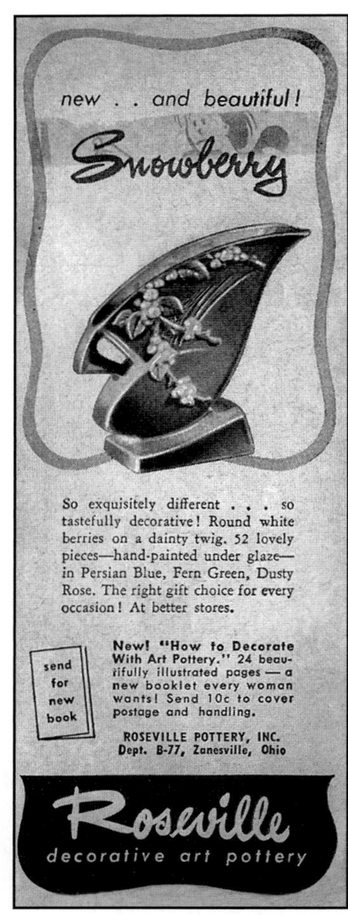

Better Homes & Gardens, July, 1947

Plate 202

Apple Blossom

Mark: Roseville in relief.

Plate 202

Row 1:

Bowl, 2½" x 6½", #326–6
- Blue....................$175.00–200.00
- Pink or Green....................$150.00–175.00

Bowl Vase, 6", #342–6
- Blue....................$250.00–275.00
- Pink or Green....................$225.00–250.00

Window Box, 2½" x 10½", #368–8
- Blue....................$200.00–225.00
- Pink or Green....................$175.00–200.00

Row 2:

Vase, 10", #388–10
- Blue....................$300.00–350.00
- Pink or Green....................$250.00–300.00

Vase, 15½", #392–15
- Blue....................$650.00–750.00
- Pink or Green....................$550.00–650.00

Vase, 12½", #390–12
- Blue....................$400.00–450.00
- Pink or Green....................$350.00–400.00

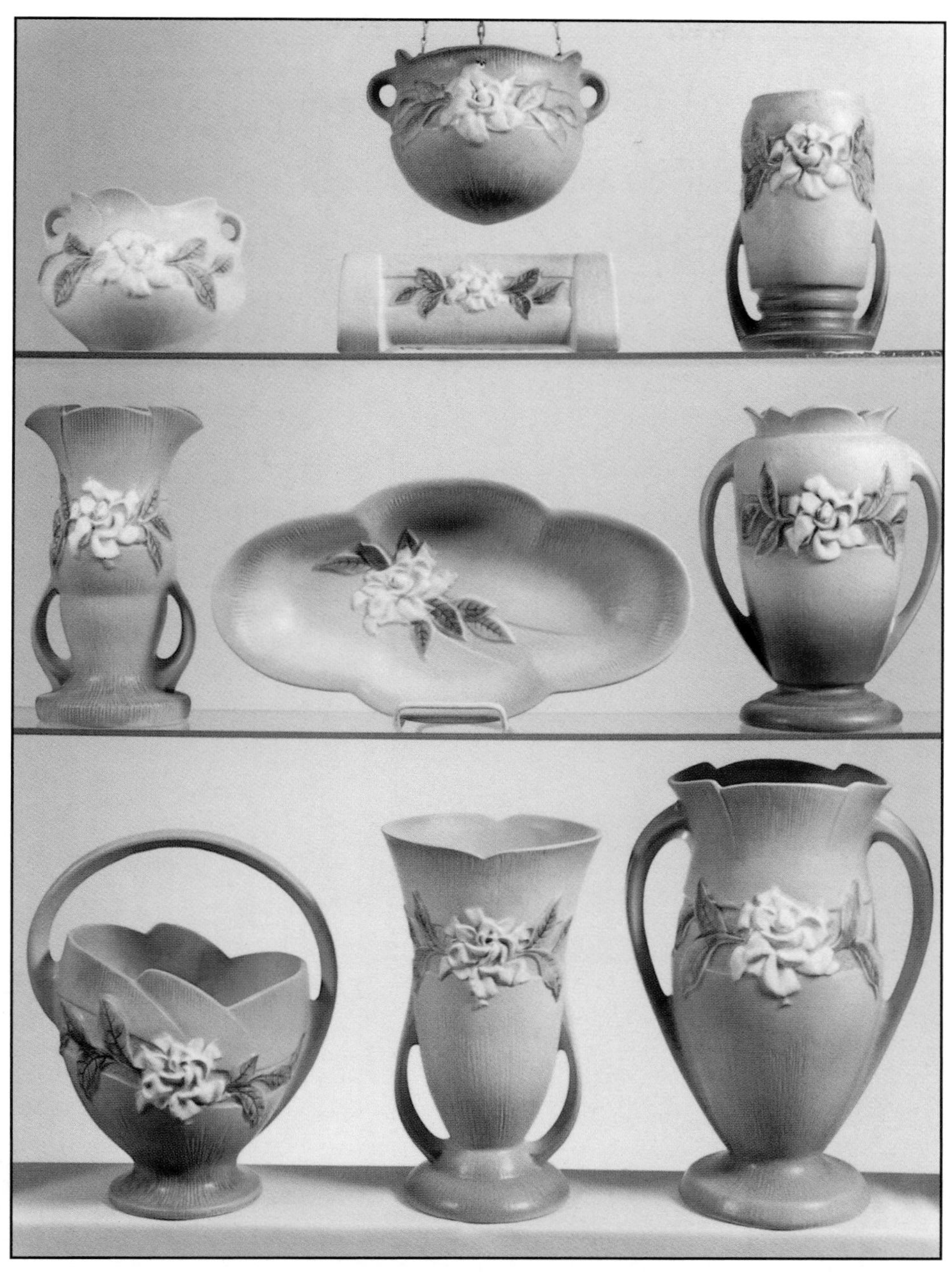

Plate 203

Gardenia

Mark: Roseville in relief.

Plate 203

Row 1:

Hanging Basket, 6", #661 .... $250.00–300.00

Bowl, 5", #641–5 .... $125.00–150.00

Window Box, 3" x 8½", #658–8 .... $100.00–125.00

Vase, 8", #683–8 .... $150.00–175.00

Row 2:

Vase, 10", #685–10 .... $175.00–225.00

Row 2 (continued):

Tray, 15", #631–14 .... $200.00–250.00

Vase, 10½", #686–10 .... $225.00–250.00

Row 3:

Basket, 12", #610–12 .... $300.00–350.00

Vase, 12", #687–12 .... $250.00–275.00

Vase, 14½", #689–14 .... $375.00–425.00

Plate 204

Mayfair

Mark: Roseville in relief.

Plate 204

Jardiniere, 7½", #90–4....................$50.00–75.00
Pitcher, 5", #1101–5........................$75.00–85.00
Pitcher, 5", #1102–5........................$75.00–85.00
Cornucopia,
3" x 6½", #1013–6..................$60.00–75.00

Mayfair

Mark: Roseville in relief.

Plate 205

Row 1:
Jardiniere, 4", #1109–4..$60.00–75.00
Planter, 3½" x 8½", #1113–8...................................$70.00–85.00

Row 2:
Flowerpot, 4½", #71–4..$70.00–85.00
Vase, 7", #1104–9..$90.00–100.00
Teapot, 5", #1121..$125.00–150.00

Row 3:
Candle Holder, 4½", #115–1, pair...........................$50.00–60.00
Bowl, 7", ...$40.00–50.00
Bowl, 10", #1119–9...$60.00–70.00
Vase, 12½", #1106–12..$90.00–110.00

Plate 205

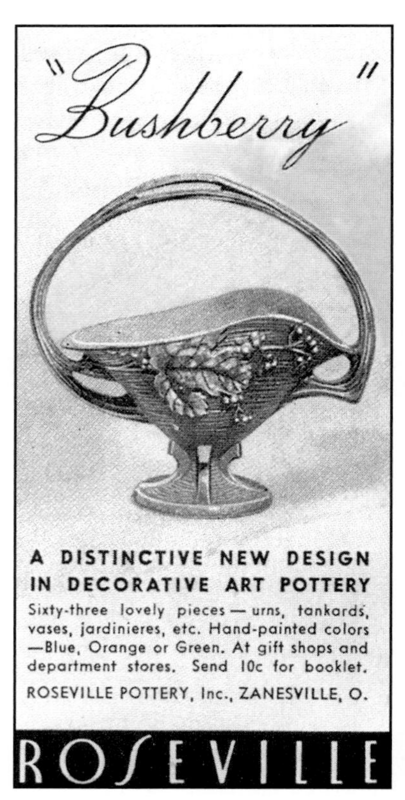

Bushberry

Mark: Roseville in relief.

Plate 206

Plate 206

Row 1:

Double Cornucopia, 6", #155–8
- Blue $200.00–225.00
- Green $175.00–200.00
- Orange $150.00–175.00

Candle Holder, 2", #1447-2CS, pair
- Blue $175.00–200.00
- Green $150.00–175.00
- Orange $125.00–150.00

Hanging Basket, 7"
- Blue $450.00–500.00
- Green $400.00–450.00
- Orange $375.00–425.00

Vase, 4", #28-4
- Blue $100.00–125.00
- Green $75.00–85.00
- Orange $65.00–75.00

Vase, 7", #32–7
- Blue $175.00–200.00
- Green $150.00–175.00
- Orange $125.00–150.00

Row 2:

Double Bud Vase, 4½", #158–4½
- Blue $175.00–200.00
- Green $150.00–175.00
- Orange $125.00–150.00

Center Bowl, 13", #385–10
- Blue $175.00–200.00
- Green $150.00–175.00
- Orange $125.00–150.00

Window Box, 6½", #383–6
- Blue $150.00–175.00
- Green $125.00–150.00
- Orange $100.00–125.00

Row 3:

Ice-Lip Pitcher, 8½", #1325
- Blue $550.00–650.00
- Green $450.00–475.00
- Orange $375.00–425.00

Mug, 3½", #1–3½
- Blue $200.00–225.00
- Green $175.00–200.00
- Orange $150.00–175.00

Vase, 6", #156–6	Blue $150.00–175.00	Green $125.00–150.00	Orange $100.00–125.00
Bud Vase, 7½", #152–7	Blue $175.00–200.00	Green $150.00–175.00	Orange $125.00–150.00
Bowl Vase, 6", #411–6	Blue $300.00–350.00	Green $250.00–275.00	Orange $225.00–250.00

Row 4:

Vase, 8", #34–8	Blue $250.00–275.00	Green $225.00–250.00	Orange $200.00–225.00
Vase, 12½", #38–12	Blue $450.00–500.00	Green $400.00–450.00	Orange $375.00–425.00
Vase, 14½", #39–14	Blue $550.00–650.00	Green $475.00–550.00	Orange $400.00–475.00
Vase, 8", #157–8	Blue $250.00–275.00	Green $225.00–250.00	Orange $200.00–225.00

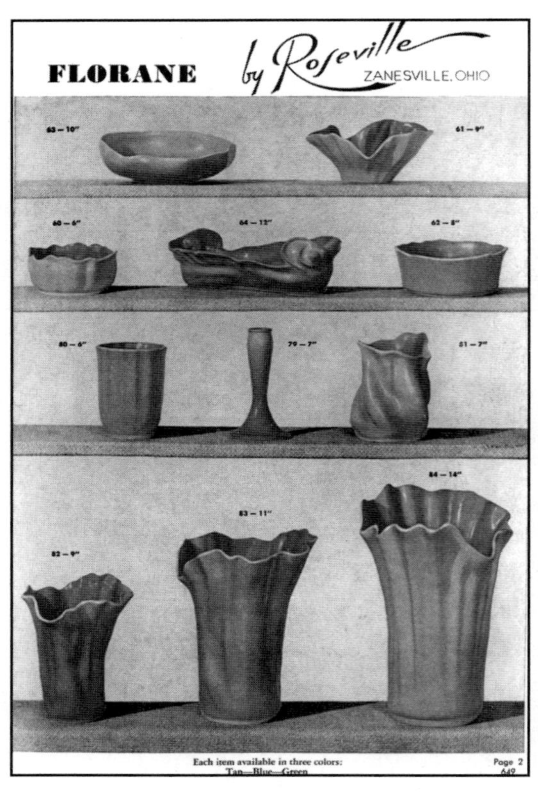

Plate 207

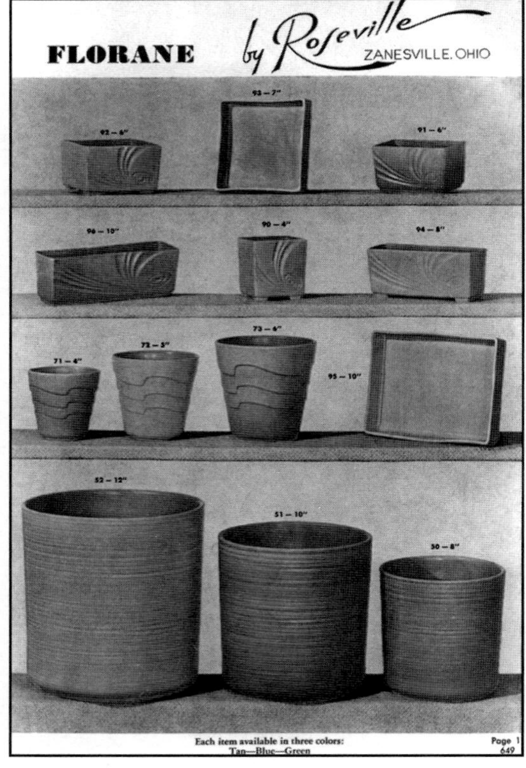

Plate 208

Florane

Marks: R or Roseville in relief.

The only item on either of these catalog pages that is at all reminiscent of the old Florane is Bud Vase, #79 (Plate 207, Row 3). The only clue as to this line's time of production is perhaps the number 649 at the bottom of both plates. We have found it not uncommon for other potteries to use a dating code of this type. The colors are very soft shades of tan, blue, and green, with a slightly deeper tan lining for contrast.

Plate 207

Row 1:

- Bowl, 10"........................$30.00–35.00
- Bowl, 9"..........................$50.00–60.00

Row 2:

- Bowl, 6"..........................$20.00–25.00
- Bowl, 12"........................$65.00–75.00
- Bowl, 8"..........................$20.00–25.00

Row 3:

- Vase, 6"...........................$30.00–35.00
- Bud Vase, 7"...................$30.00–35.00
- Vase, 7"...........................$40.00–45.00

Row 4:

- Vase, 9"...........................$75.00–90.00
- Vase, 11".......................$75.00–100.00
- Vase, 14"......................$90.00–115.00

Plate 208

Row 1:

- Planter Box, 6"..............$25.00–30.00
- Bowl, 7"..........................$20.00–25.00
- Planter, 6"......................$25.00–30.00

Row 2:

- Planter, 10"....................$45.00–50.00
- Planter, 4"......................$20.00–25.00
- Planter, 8"......................$35.00–40.00

Row 3:

- Pot, 4"............................$20.00–25.00
- Pot, 5"............................$25.00–30.00
- Pot, 6"............................$35.00–40.00
- Bowl, 10".......................$25.00–30.00

Row 4:

- Sand Jar, 12".............$100.00–135.00
- Jar, 10".......................$100.00–125.00
- Jar, 8"..........................$90.00–115.00

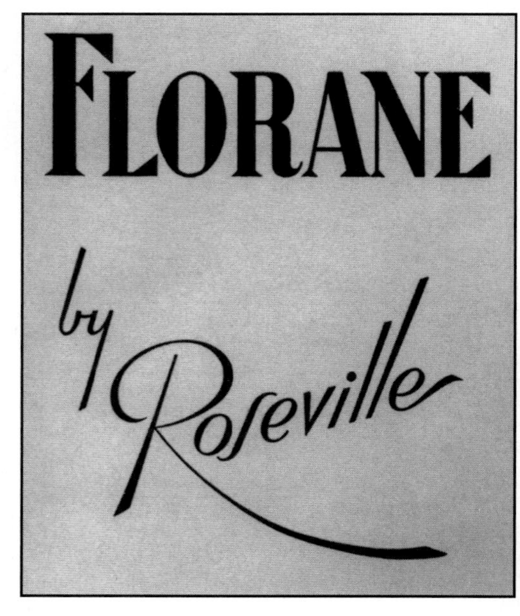

Wincraft

Mark: Roseville in relief.

Plate 209

Vase, 7", #274–7 .... $175.00–225.00
Basket, 12", #210–12 .... $450.00–500.00

Plate 210

Row 1:
Cornucopia, 9" x 5", #221–8 .... $125.00–150.00
Dealer Sign, 4½" x 8" $4,000.00–4,500.00
Mug, 4½" $75.00–100.00

Row 2:
Center Bowl,
4" x 13½", #227–10 .... $125.00–150.00
Bookends, 6½", #259, pair $150.00–175.00

Row 3:
Vase, 16", #288–15 .... $325.00–375.00
Ewer, 19", #218–18 .... $450.00–550.00

Plate 209

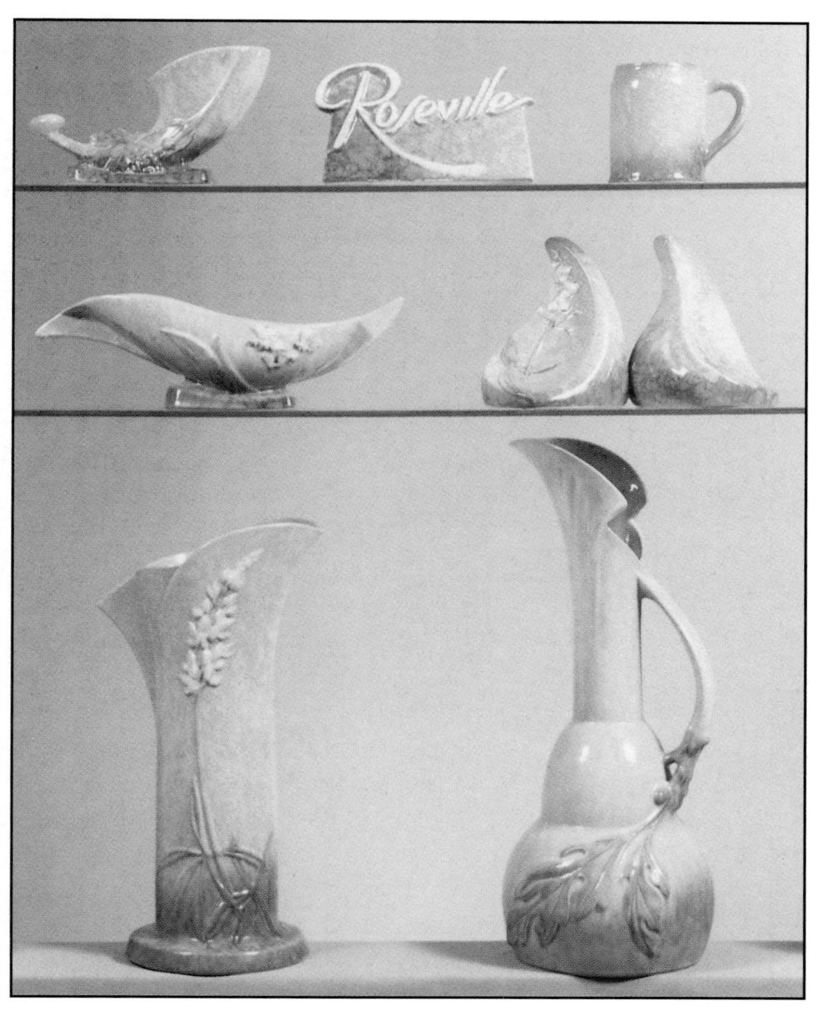

Plate 210

Better Homes & Gardens,
November, 1948

Artwood

Mark: Roseville in relief.

Plate 211

Row 1:

3-pc. Planter Set; Side sections, 4", #1050; Center section, 6", #1051–6....................$110.00–125.00

Planter, 6½" x 8½", #1054–8½..........................$85.00–95.00

Row 2:

Planter, 7" x 9½", #1055–9..............................$85.00–95.00

Vase, 8", #1057–8.......................$85.00–95.00

Planter, 6½" x 10½", #1056–10............................$85.00–95.00

Plate 211

Company placard

Good Housekeeping, December, 1949.

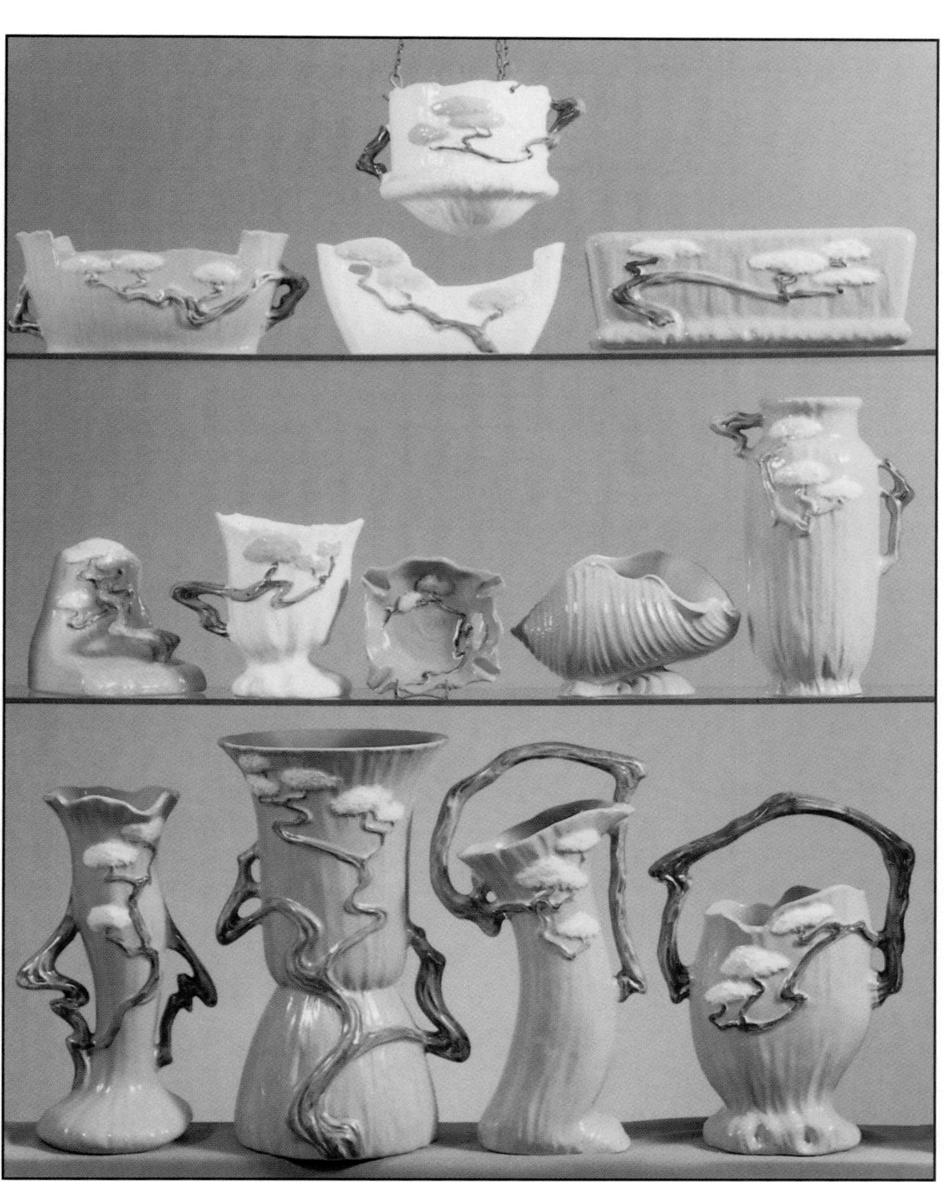

Plate 212

Ming Tree

Mark: Roseville in relief.

Plate 212

Row 1:

- Hanging Basket, 6", U.S.A. $225.00–250.00
- Bowl, 4" x 11½", #526–9....$95.00–110.00
- Planter, 4" x 8½"....$95.00–110.00
- Window Box, 4" x 11", #569–10....$125.00–150.00

Row 2:

- Bookend, 5½", #559, pair....$200.00–235.00
- Vase, 6½", #572–6....$95.00–110.00
- Ashtray, 6", #599....$75.00–85.00

Row 2 (continued):

- Conch Shell, 8½", #563....$90.00–110.00
- Vase, 10½", #583–10....$175.00–200.00

Row 3:

- Vase, 12½", #584–12....$225.00–250.00
- Vase, 14½", #585–14....$400.00–450.00
- Basket, 14½", #510–14....$275.00–300.00
- Basket, 13", #509–12....$275.00–300.00

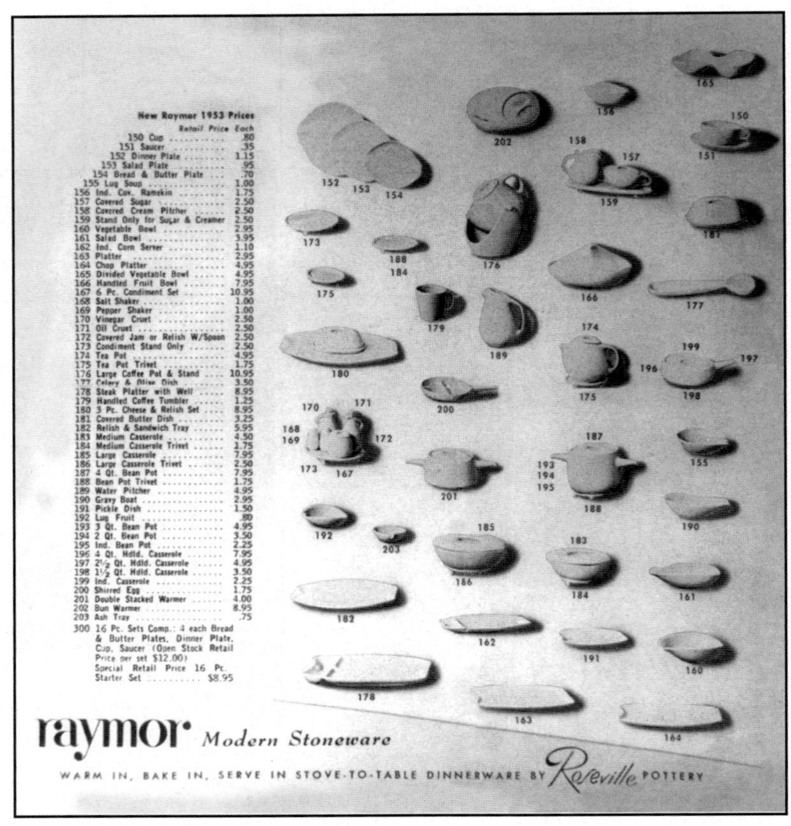

New Raymor 1953 Prices

No.	Item	Retail Price Each
150	Cup	.80
151	Saucer	.35
152	Dinner Plate	1.15
153	Salad Plate	.95
154	Bread & Butter Plate	.70
155	Lug Soup	1.00
156	Ind. Cov. Ramekin	1.75
157	Covered Sugar	2.50
158	Covered Cream Pitcher	2.50
159	Stand Only for Sugar & Creamer	2.50
160	Vegetable Bowl	2.95
161	Salad Bowl	3.95
162	Ind. Corn Server	1.10
163	Platter	2.95
164	Chop Platter	4.95
165	Divided Vegetable Bowl	4.95
166	Handled Fruit Bowl	7.95
167	6 Pc. Condiment Set	10.95
168	Salt Shaker	1.00
169	Pepper Shaker	1.00
170	Vinegar Cruet	2.50
171	Oil Cruet	2.50
172	Covered Jam or Relish W/Spoon	2.50
173	Condiment Stand Only	2.50
174	Tea Pot	4.95
175	Tea Pot Trivet	1.75
176	Large Coffee Pot & Stand	10.95
177	Celery & Olive Dish	3.50
178	Steak Platter with Well	8.95
179	Handled Coffee Tumbler	1.25
180	3 Pc. Cheese & Relish Set	8.95
181	Covered Butter Dish	3.25
182	Relish & Sandwich Tray	5.95
183	Medium Casserole	4.50
184	Medium Casserole Trivet	1.75
185	Large Casserole	7.95
186	Large Casserole Trivet	2.50
187	4 Qt. Bean Pot	7.95
188	Bean Pot Trivet	1.75
189	Water Pitcher	4.95
190	Gravy Boat	2.95
191	Pickle Dish	1.50
192	Lug Fruit	.80
193	3 Qt. Bean Pot	4.95
194	2 Qt. Bean Pot	3.50
195	Ind. Bean Pot	2.25
196	4 Qt. Hdld. Casserole	7.95
197	2½ Qt. Hdld. Casserole	4.95
198	1½ Qt. Hdld. Casserole	3.50
199	Ind. Casserole	2.25
200	Shirred Egg	1.75
201	Double Stacked Warmer	4.00
202	Bun Warmer	8.95
203	Ash Tray	.75
300	16 Pc. Sets Comp.: 4 each Bread & Butter Plates, Dinner Plate, Cup, Saucer (Open Stock Retail Price per set $12.00) Special Retail Price 16 Pc. Starter Set	$8.95

raymor *Modern Stoneware*

WARM IN, BAKE IN, SERVE IN STOVE-TO-TABLE DINNERWARE BY Roseville POTTERY

Plate 213

Raymor

Mark: Raymor by Roseville, USA, in relief.

Plate 213

Row 1:

- Gravy Boat, 9½", #190 .... $30.00–35.00
- Salad Bowl, 11½", #161 .... $35.00–40.00
- Glass Tumblers, 4½",
  - shown bottom of opposite page $35.00–40.00

Row 2:

- Individual Casserole, 7½", #199 .... $40.00–45.00
- Individual Corn Server, 12½", #162 .... $45.00–50.00
- Shirred Egg, 10", #200 .... $40.00–45.00

Row 3:

- Individual Covered Ramekin, 6½", #156 .... $35.00–40.00
- Divided Vegetable Bowl, 13", #165 .... $55.00–65.00
- Covered Butter, 7½", #181 .... $75.00–100.00

Row 4:

- Handled Coffee Tumbler, 4",
  - series of #s denote trial color $40.00–50.00
- Condiment Set — Tray, 8½" $40.00–50.00
  - Cruet, 5½" $65.00–75.00
  - Mustard, 3½" $50.00–60.00
  - Salt and Pepper, 3½" $30.00–35.00
- Large Casserole, 13½",
  - add $25.00 for lid $85.00–95.00

Row 5:

- Vegetable, 9", #160 .... $30.00–40.00
- Water Pitcher, 10", #189 .... $100.00–150.00
- Medium Casserole, 11", #183 .... $75.00–85.00

raymor
modern artware
by Roseville
28-8
U.S.A.

Plate 214

Raymor Modern Artware

Mark: Illustrated above.

Plate 214
Row 1:
Vase, 6½", ...$500.00–600.00
Bowl, 3" x 7", #41–6 ....$300.00–350.00

Assorted Items

Row 2:
Ashtray, Souvenir of
plant tours, 3½" $25.00–35.00
CAPRI, 10", #533–10 ....$40.00–50.00
CAPRI Square Dish, 4" x 2", #552 ....$25.00–35.00
Ashtray, Souvenir
of plant tours, 3½"..................................$25.00–35.00
Row 3
Wall Pocket, 10½", #711 ....$250.00–300.00
CAPRI Vase, 12½", #593–12 ....$150.00–175.00
Star, 2" x 10", #713...$75.00–100.00
Row 4:
Teapot, 6½", #14..$125.00–150.00
Cookie Jar, 10", #20...$200.00–225.00
Mixing Bowl, 5½", #11–8 ....$40.00–50.00

Plate 215

Plate 215
Mixing Bowl, 9", #11–8................................$55.00–65.00
Mixing Bowl, 8", #10 ....$45.00–55.00
Mixing Bowl, 7", #10–6................................$35.00–45.00

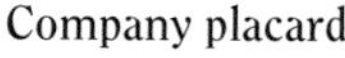
Company placard

Plate 216

Silhouette
Mark: Roseville in relief.

Plate 216

Row 1:

Box, 4½", #740 .... $150.00–175.00

Double Planter, 5½", #757–9 .... $125.00–150.00

Ewer, 6½", #716–6 .... $100.00–125.00

Row 2:

Vase, 6", #781–6 .... $90.00–110.00

Row 2 (continued):

Vase, 8", #784–8 .... $100.00–125.00

Vase, 14", #789–14 .... $350.00–400.00

Vase, 10", #787–10, with nude $750.00–850.00

Vase, 6", #780–6 .... $90.00–110.00

Plate 217

Lotus
Mark: Roseville in relief.

Plate 217

Planter, 3½" x 4", #L9–4 .... $100.00–125.00

Pillow Vase, 10½", #L4–10 .... $275.00–325.00

Bowl, 3" x 9", #L6–9 .... $150.00–175.00

Plate 218

Mock Orange

Marks: Roseville U.S.A., Mock Orange, in relief, and gold and green foil label (see illustration).

Plate 218
Row 1:
- Window Box, 8½" x 4½", #956–8 .... $100.00–125.00
- Planter, 3½" x 9, #931–8 .... $125.00–150.00
- Planter, 4" x 10½", #932 .... $125.00–150.00

Row 2:
- Vase, 8½", #973–8 .... $150.00–175.00
- Vase, 13", #985–12 .... $350.00–450.00
- Pillow Vase, 7", #930–8 .... $150.00–175.00

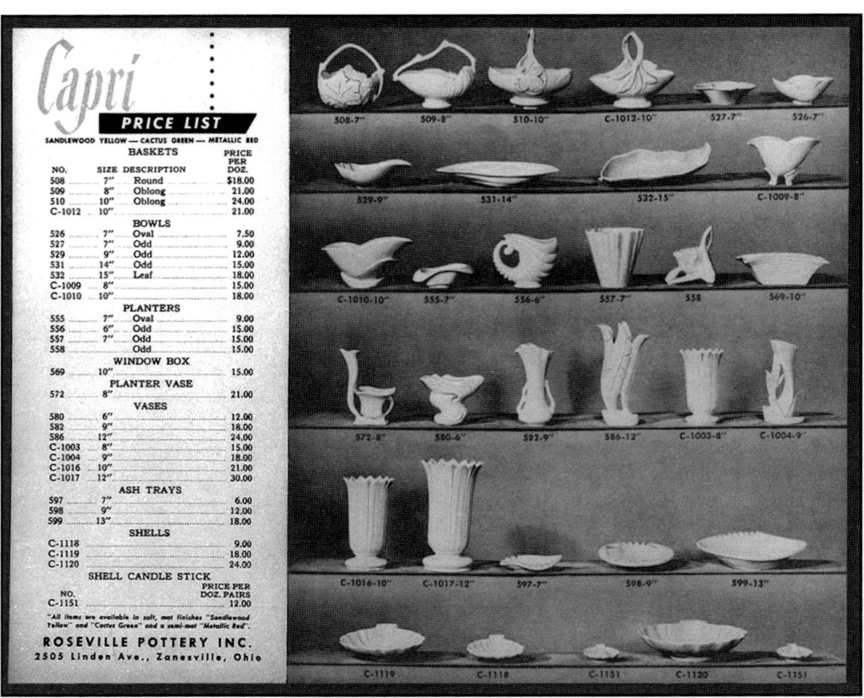

Capri

PRICE LIST

SANDLEWOOD YELLOW — CACTUS GREEN — METALLIC RED

NO.	SIZE	DESCRIPTION	PRICE PER DOZ.
		BASKETS	
508	7"	Round	$18.00
509	8"	Oblong	21.00
510	10"	Oblong	24.00
C-1012	10"		21.00
		BOWLS	
526	7"	Oval	7.50
527	7"	Odd	9.00
529	9"	Odd	12.00
531	14"	Odd	15.00
532	15"	Leaf	18.00
C-1009	8"		15.00
C-1010	10"		18.00
		PLANTERS	
555	7"	Oval	9.00
556	6"	Odd	15.00
557	7"	Odd	15.00
558		Odd	15.00
		WINDOW BOX	
569	10"		15.00
		PLANTER VASE	
572	8"		21.00
		VASES	
580	6"		12.00
582	9"		18.00
586	12"		24.00
C-1003	8"		15.00
C-1004	9"		18.00
C-1016	10"		21.00
C-1017	12"		30.00
		ASH TRAYS	
597	7"		6.00
598	9"		12.00
599	13"		18.00
		SHELLS	
C-1118			9.00
C-1119			18.00
C-1120			24.00

SHELL CANDLE STICK

NO.	PRICE PER DOZ. PAIRS
C-1151	12.00

"All items are available in soft, mat finishes "Sandlewood Yellow" and "Cactus Green" and a semi-mat "Metallic Red".

ROSEVILLE POTTERY INC.
2505 Linden Ave., Zanesville, Ohio

Mock Orange

Plate 219

Plate 220

Royal Capri

Mark: Roseville in relief.

Plate 219

Leaf, 2" x 10½", #533–10 ....$200.00–225.00
Vase, 9", #583–9..............................$250.00–275.00

Capri

Mark: Roseville in relief.

Plate 220

Row 1:
Leaf, 16", #532–16 ....$35.00–45.00
Leaf, 15", #531–14 ....$35.00–45.00
Row 2:
Window Box,
3" x 10", #569–10..........................$45.00–55.00
Planter, 5" x 10½",
#C–1010–10 ....$45.00–55.00
Row 3:
Bowl, 9", #529–9..................................$20.00–30.00
Ashtray, 9", #598–9..............................$40.00–50.00
Bowl, 7", #527–7.................................$20.00–30.00
Row 4:
Planter, 7", #558 ....$85.00–95.00
Shell, 13½", #C–1120...........................$50.00–60.00
Vase, 9", #582–9...................................$50.00–60.00

Plate 221

Assorted Items

Mark: Roseville in relief.

Plate 221

Row 1:
- Leaf Dish, 10½", #533–10, CAPRI shape $45.00–55.00
- Basket, 7", #508–7, CAPRI shape $150.00–175.00

Row 2:
- CAPRI Bowl, 7", #527–7 .... $30.00–40.00
- CAPRI Cornucopia, 6", #556–6 .... $85.00–95.00
- CRYSTAL GREEN Bowl, 7", #357–6, seldom seen line $100.00–125.00

Row 3:
- HYDE PARK Ashtray, 8½", Made in U.S.A., #1900 .... $30.00–40.00
- BURMESE Candlesticks, 3", #75–B, pair $40.00–50.00
- BURMESE Planter, 10", #908–10 .... $50.00–60.00

Row 4:
- Ashtray, 13", #599–13, black glaze, CAPRI shape $50.00–60.00
- Ashtray, 13", #204–13 .... $50.00–60.00
  Made from Roseville molds after pottery closed by a Connecticut firm.

Assorted Items

Plate 222

Row 1:

Ashtray, 8½", Vernco, #1925 ....$30.00–40.00
Ashtray, 5½", The Hyde Park, #1915 ...$30.00–40.00
Ashtray, Made in U.S.A., #1950 ....$30.00–40.00

Row 2:

Tray, 8", Created Cal Art $40.00–50.00
Planter, 4", Cal Art Creations, #1510
by Roseville, U.S.A........................$40.00–45.00
Section of 5-part relish, 9½" x 5½",
#1507 ....$15.00–20.00

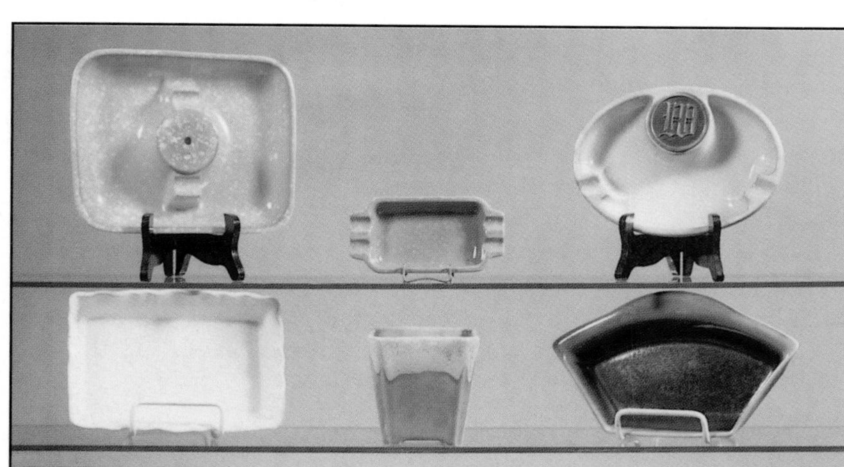

Plate 222

Pasadena

Mark: Roseville Pasadena Planter.

Plate 223

Planter, 9" x 3½", #L–17.......................$40.00–45.00
Planter, 6½" x 5½", #L–38 ....$60.00–70.00
Planter, 3½" x 10½", #L–35 ....$65.00–75.00

Raymor, Vernco, Cal Art, Hyde Park, and Pasadena were companies for whom Roseville produced specially ordered wares.

Plate 223

Kettle and Skillet Set

Plate 224

This 3-piece Kettle and Skillet set was found in its original carton. It may be found in matt black or blue and white mottled glazing.

Bowl, 2" x 5", #1797 ....$30.00–40.00
Skillet/Ashtray, 6½", #1799 ....$35.00–45.00
Pot, #1798 ....$30.00–40.00

Add $10.00 to each for blue.
Box, $50.00–75.00

On reverse side the box reads: Kettle and Skillet Set, packaged by H. Bettis Co. (This Zanesville Co. later became Grief Bros.)

Plate 224

Plate 225

Wall Pockets, Masks, Sconces

Plate 225

Row 1:

CHLORON, Boy, 9½" $8,000.00–9,000.00
CHLORON, Corner Vase, 17" $4,000.00–5,000.00
CHLORON, Girl, 9½" $8,000.00–9,000.00

Row 2:

CHLORON, 11½" $1,500.00–2,000.00
CHLORON, Sconce, 12½" x 12" $4,000.00–5,000.00

Row 2 (continued):

CHLORON, 11" $1,250.00–1,500.00

Row 3:

ANTIQUE MATT GREEN, 10" $450.00–500.00
MATT GREEN, 11" $350.00–400.00

Plate 226

Wall Pockets, Sconces

Plate 226

Row 1:

CHLORON Sconce, 17" $5,000.00–6,000.00

CHLORON Sconce, 12" $3,000.00–4,000.00

CHLORON Sconce, 17", trial glaze $7,000.00–8,000.00

Row 2:

MATT GREEN, Wall Pocket, 15" $650.00–750.00

Row 2 (continued):

CHLORON Letter Receiver, 15½" $5,000.00–6,000.00

CHLORON Sconce, 10" $3,000.00–4,000.00

Row 3:

CHLORON, with nude, 8½" $3,500.00–4,500.00

CHLORON, Wall Pocket, 8" $3,500.00–4,500.00

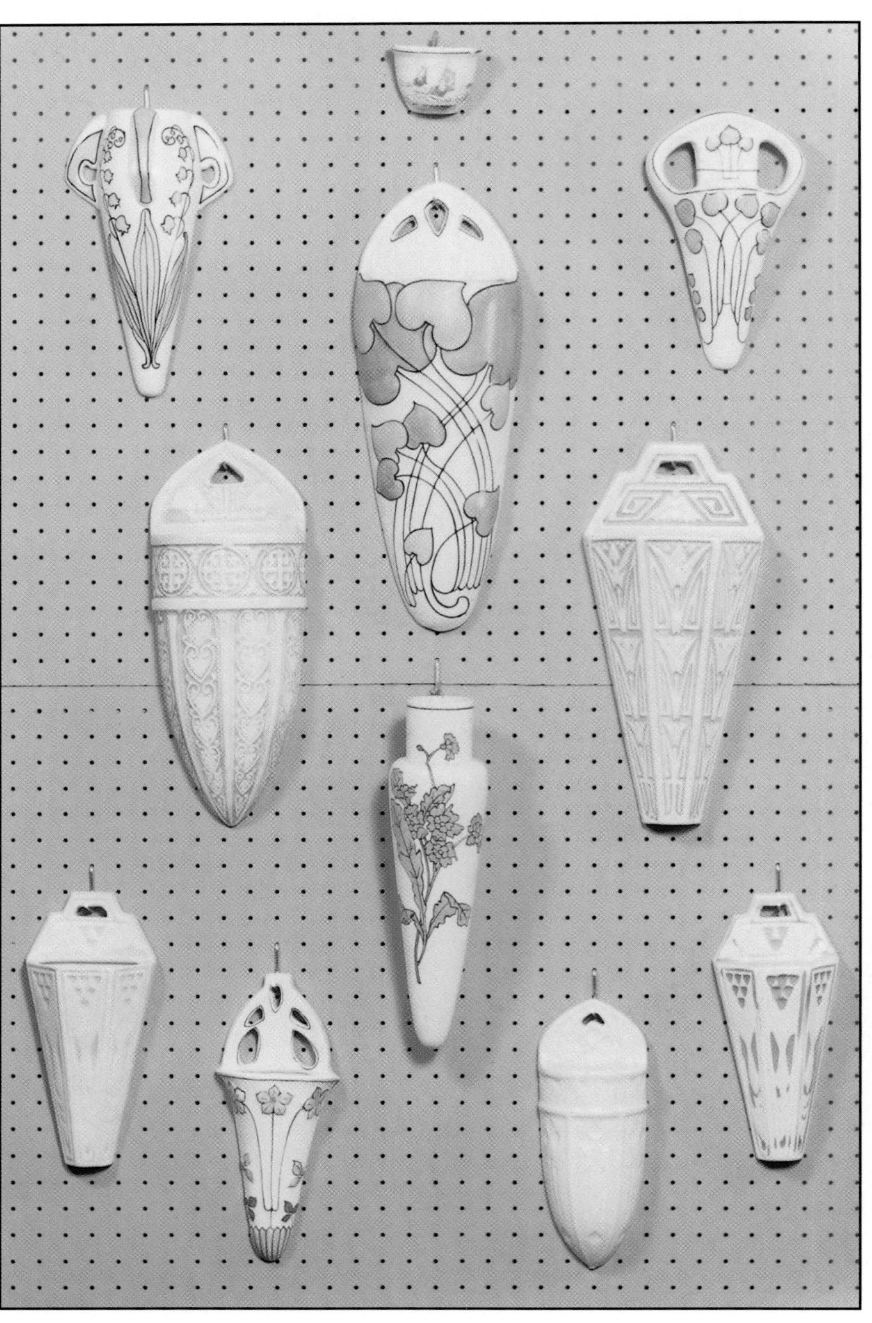

Plate 227

Wall Pockets

Plate 227

Top center:
- LANDSCAPE, 2½" $800.00–900.00

Row 1:
- PERSIAN, 11" $500.00–600.00
- CERAMIC DESIGN, 17" $800.00–900.00
- CERAMIC DESIGN, 10" $400.00–450.00

Row 2:
- PINK TINT, 14½" $500.00–600.00
- PERSIAN, 13½" $1,500.00–2,000.00
- GREEN TINT, 14½" $450.00–550.00

Row 3:
- YELLOW TINT, 10" $200.00–225.00
- CERAMIC DESIGN, 11" $400.00–450.00
- IVORY I, 10" $250.00–300.00
- GREEN TINT, 10" $250.00–300.00

There is a very fine line drawn between the identification of some of these early wall pockets. Indeed in the Roseville catalogs, some lines were designated "Ceramic Design" on one page — "Decorated" on another. And that term in itself was sometimes applied to the Persian line, which was in some instances called "Decorated Persian." Gold Traced...Decorated and Gold Traced — in that reference was "Decorated" again Persian? It looks the same! There are two types of decoration, you will notice — one is molded decoration, the other is not. Since we know that Persian was not molded, we associate this decorated type with the Persian line. To make a distinction between the two, the molded could be called Ceramic Design, without actually being incorrect.

Wall Pockets, Carnelian I

Plate 228

Row 1:

9½" $200.00–250.00
8" $200.00–250.00
8" $200.00–250.00
8" $200.00–250.00

Wall Pockets, Carnelian II

Row 2:

8" $350.00–400.00
8" $350.00–400.00
8" $350.00–400.00
8" $350.00–400.00

Wall Pockets

Row 3:

AZURINE, ORCHID, AND TURQUOISE
10" $175.00–225.00
ROSECRAFT BLUE,
10½" $175.00–225.00
ROSECRAFT BLACK,
9"..................................$175.00–225.00
ROSECRAFT YELLOW,
10"................................$175.00–225.00

Row 4:

MOSTIQUE, 9½"..................$350.00–400.00
VOLPATO, 8½"....................$650.00–750.00
VELMOSS SCROLL,
11"................................$375.00–450.00
ROZANE 1917,
7½" $350.00–400.00

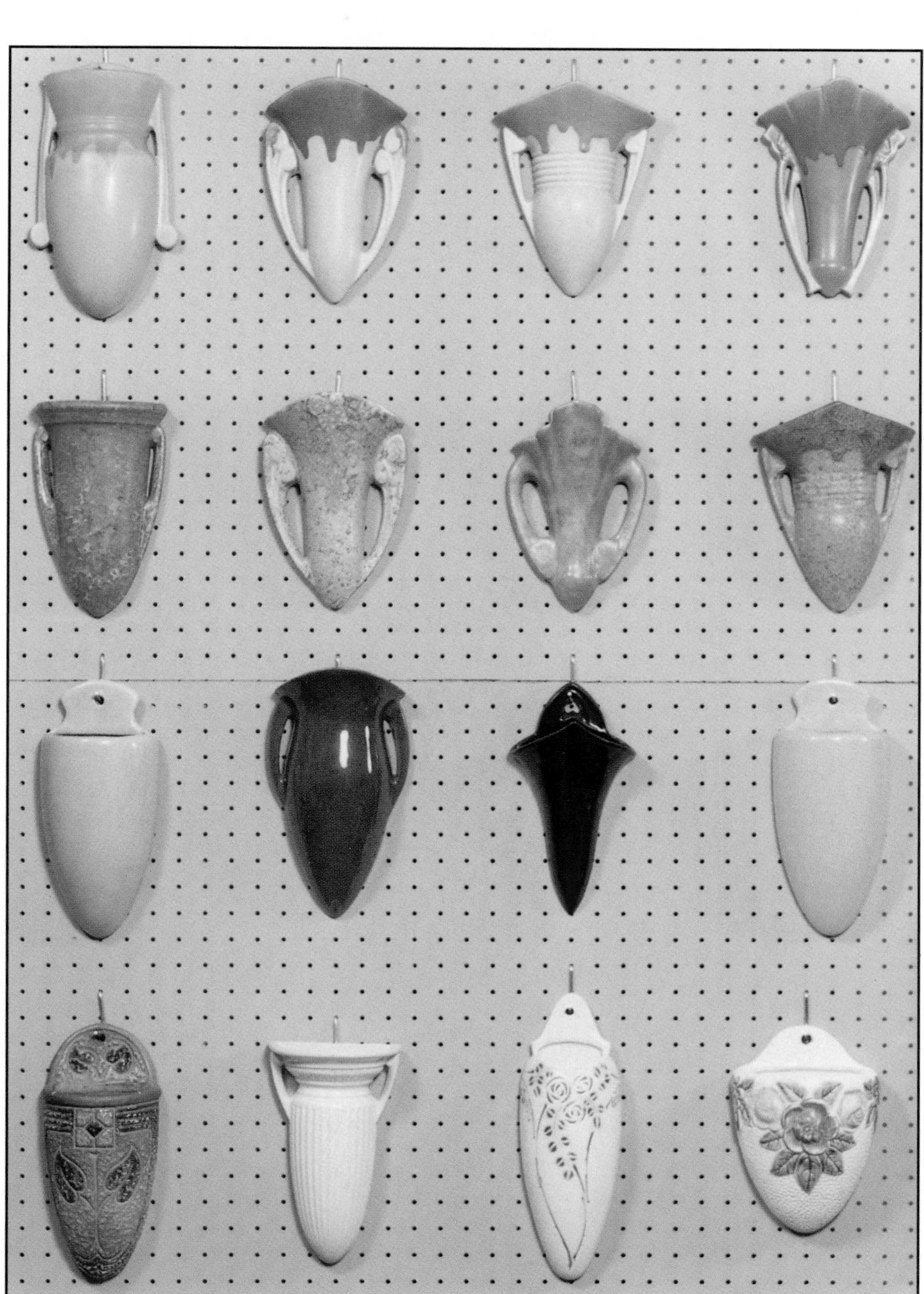

Plate 228

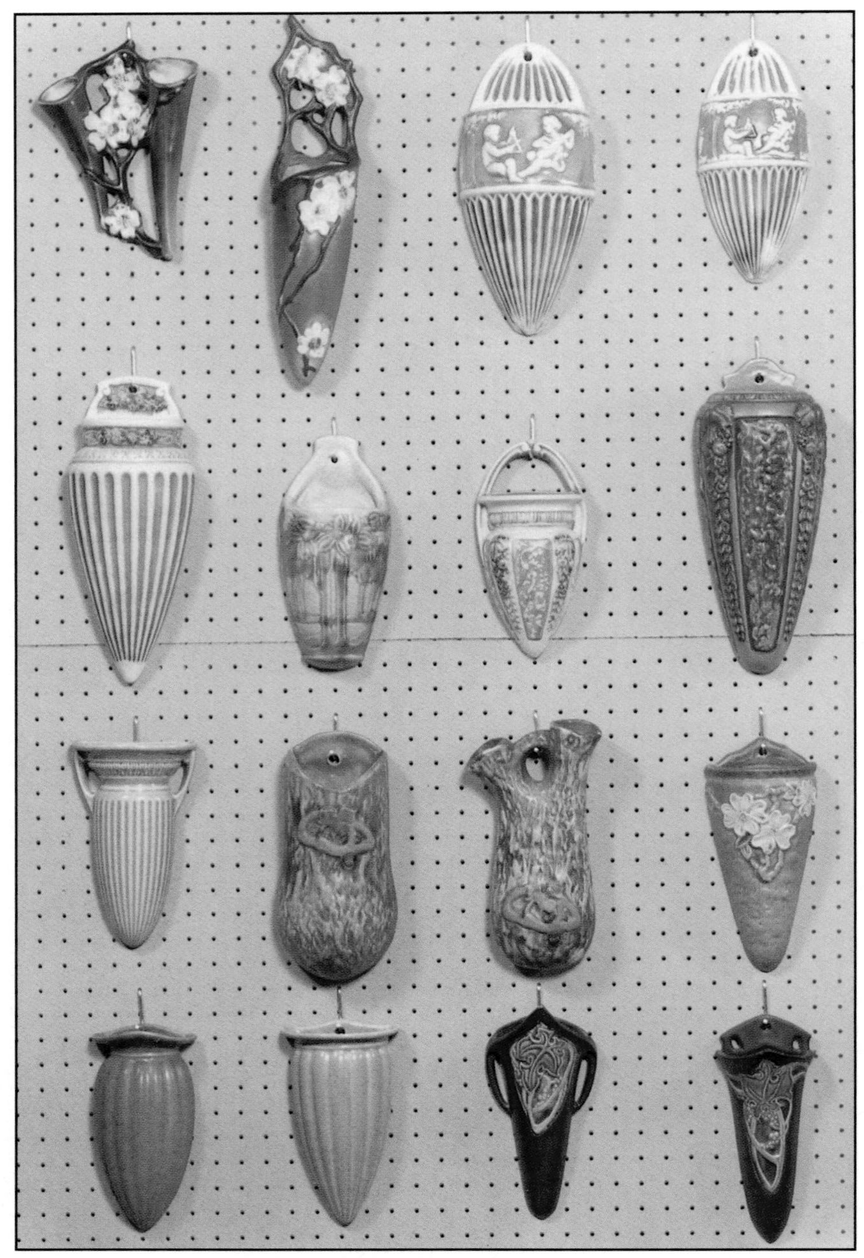

Plate 229

Wall Pockets

Plate 229

Row 1:

DOGWOOD I, 9" $350.00–400.00
DOGWOOD I, 15" $1,000.00–1,250.00
DONATELLO, 11½"..$250.00–275.00
DONATELLO, 9" $175.00–200.00

Row 2:

CORINTHIAN, 12" $300.00–350.00
VISTA, 9½", with excellent mold/color $900.00–1,000.00
Ivory FLORENTINE, 8½", #1238...................$1,000.00–1,100.00
FLORENTINE, 12½" $300.00–350.00

Row 3:

SAVONA, 8"..$750.00–850.00
IMPERIAL I, 10" $250.00–300.00
IMPERIAL I, 10" $250.00–300.00
DOGWOOD II, 9½"..$275.00–300.00

Row 4:

LOMBARDY, 8", matt glaze...................................$250.00–275.00
LOMBARDY, 8", glossy glaze $250.00–275.00
ROSECRAFT VINTAGE, 9"....................................$350.00–400.00
ROSECRAFT VINTAGE, 9"....................................$400.00–450.00

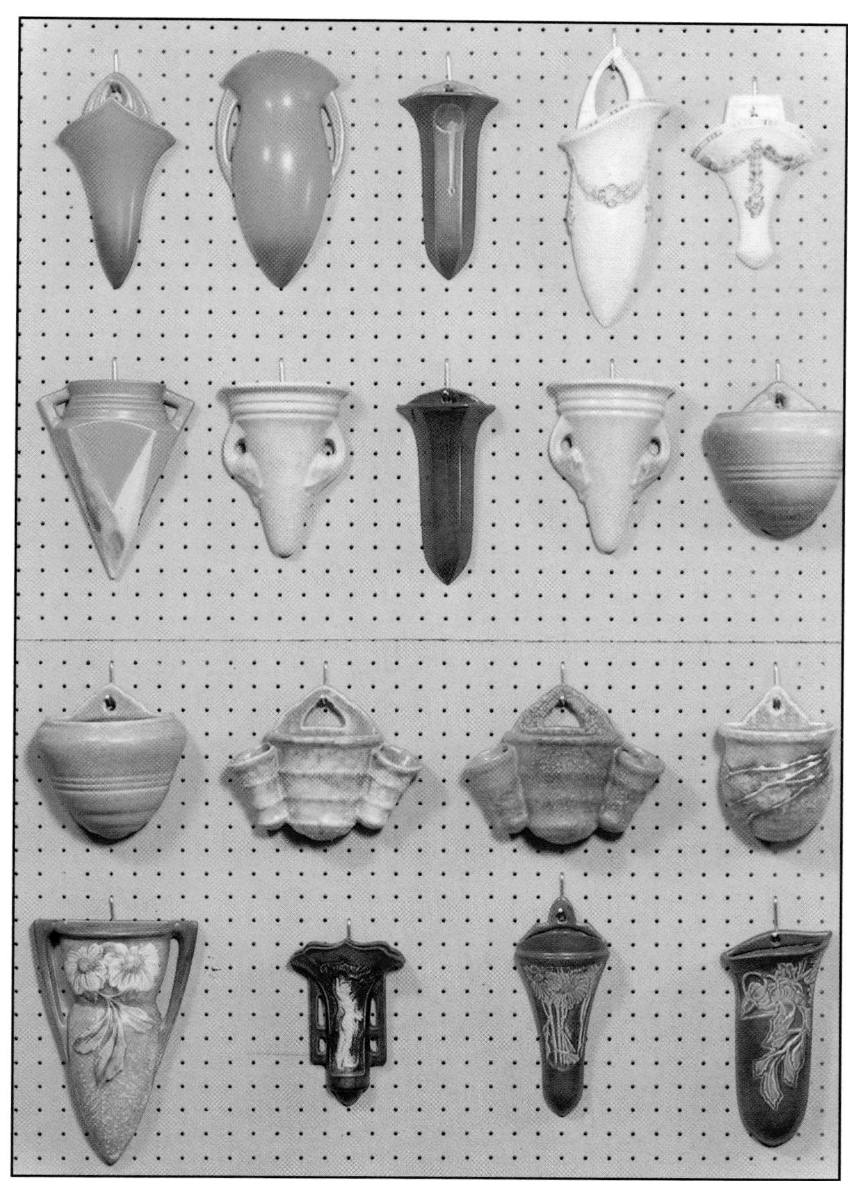

Plate 230

Wall Pockets

Plate 230

Row 1:

FLORANE, 9" $175.00–225.00
FLORANE, 10½" $225.00–275.00
ROSECRAFT HEXAGON, 8½" $450.00–500.00
LA ROSE, 12" $350.00–400.00
LA ROSE, 7½" $200.00–250.00

Row 2:

FUTURA, 8" $500.00–600.00
TUSCANY, 7", blue glaze $275.00–325.00
ROSECRAFT HEXAGON, 8½"
note blue glaze $1,250.00–1,500.00
TUSCANY, 7" $275.00–325.00
EARLAM, 6½" $750.00–850.00

Row 3:

IMPERIAL II, 6½" $800.00–900.00
IMPERIAL II, 6½", trial glaze $3,000.00–4,000.00
IMPERIAL II, 6½" $550.00–650.00
IMPERIAL II, 6½" $650.00–700.00

Row 4:

DAHLROSE, 10" $300.00–350.00
ROSECRAFT PANEL, 7" $550.00–650.00
ROSECRAFT PANEL, 9" $350.00–400.00
ROSECRAFT PANEL, 9" $400.00–450.00

Plate 231

Wall Pockets

Plate 231

Row 1:

- BLACKBERRY, 8½" $1,500.00–1,700.00
- SUNFLOWER, 7½" $1,400.00–1,600.00
- WISTERIA, 8"
  - tan $1,200.00–1,400.00
  - blue $1,400.00–1,600.00

Row 2:

- VELMOSS, 8½"
  - green $1,000.00–1,250.00
  - red, blue or tan $1,500.00–2,000.00
- FERELLA, 6½"
  - pink $1,500.00–1,750.00
  - brown $1,250.00–1,500.00
- BANEDA, 8"
  - pink $3,000.00–3,500.00
  - green $2,500.00–3,000.00
- JONQUIL, 8½" $800.00–900.00
- MORNING GLORY, 8½"
  - green $1,250.00–1,500.00
  - white $1,000.00–1,250.00

Row 3:

- CHERRY BLOSSOM, 8"
  - pink $1,200.00–1,400.00
  - brown $600.00–700.00
- THORN APPLE Bucket, 8½" $900.00–1,000.00
- MOSS Bucket, 10" $600.00–700.00
- LUFFA, 8½" $700.00–800.00

Row 4:

- THORN APPLE, 8",
- #1280–8, standard $500.00–600.00
- ORIAN, 8", blue, tan, red $800.00–900.00
  - yellow $1,000.00–1,200.00
- MOSS, 8", #1278–8 .... $550.00–650.00

Wall Pockets, Plates, Shelves

Plate 232

Row 1:

PEONY, 8", #1293–8 .... $300.00–350.00
IRIS, 8", #1284–8 .... $550.00–650.00
FUCHSIA, 8½", #1282–8
 blue $700.00–800.00
 brown or green $500.00–600.00
BLEEDING HEART, 8½", #1287–8 .... $500.00–550.00

Row 2:

PRIMROSE, 8½", #1277–8
 blue $600.00–700.00
 tan or pink $450.00–550.00
POPPY, 8½", #1281-8
 pink $800.00–900.00
 gray or green $500.00–550.00
COSMOS, 8½", #1286–8
 blue or green $550.00–650.00
 tan $450.00–550.00

Row 3:

PINE CONE, 8½", #466
 blue $600.00–700.00
 brown $500.00–600.00
 green $350.00–400.00
PINE CONE Plate, 7½", foil sticker
 blue $750.00–850.00
 brown $600.00–700.00
 green $350.00–400.00
PINE CONE Bucket, 9", #1283
 blue $1,000.00–1,100.00
 brown $600.00–700.00
 *green $900.00–1,000.00

Row 4:

PINE CONE Wall Shelf, #1
 blue $600.00–700.00
 brown $475.00–525.00
 *green $400.00–450.00
PINE CONE, 8½", #1273–8
 blue $550.00–650.00
 brown $450.00–500.00
 green $375.00–425.00
IVORY II, 8½", #1273-8 .... $350.00–450.00
IVORY II Shelf, 5½", #8 .... $125.00–175.00

*Green is harder to find in these shapes than brown.

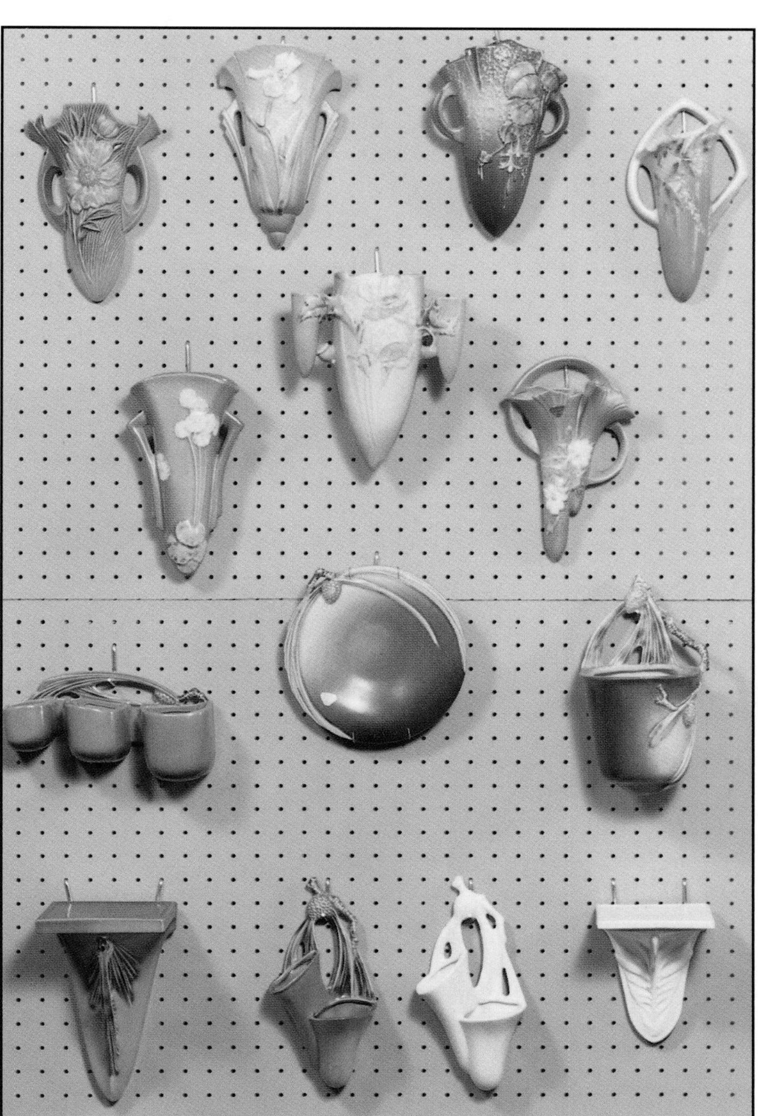

Plate 232

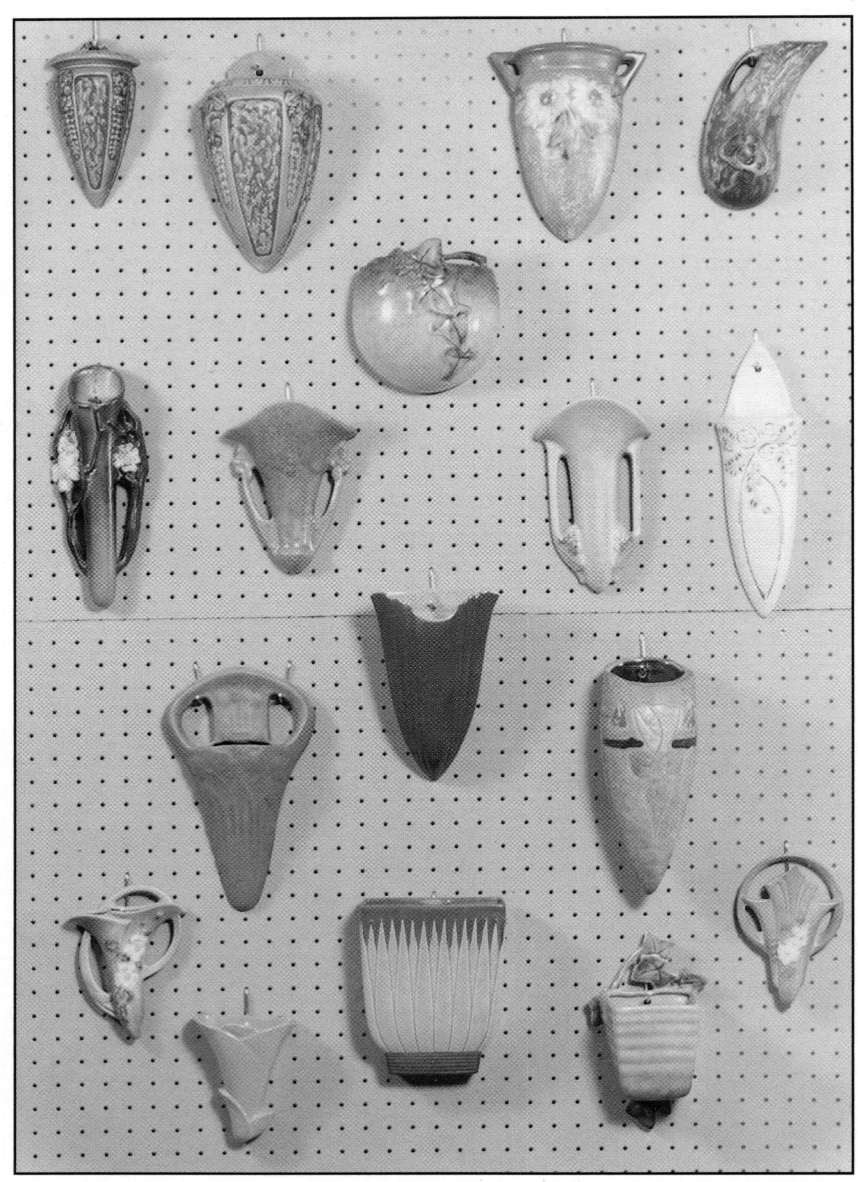

Plate 233

Wall Pockets

Plate 233
Row 1:
FLORENTINE, 7" $100.00–125.00
FLORENTINE, 9½" $125.00–150.00
DAHLROSE, 9" $125.00–150.00
IMPERIAL I, 8" $250.00–275.00
Row 2:
WINCRAFT, 5", #267–5 ....$200.00–225.00
Row 3:
DOGWOOD I, 10" $375.00–425.00
CARNELIAN II, 7" $350.00–375.00
TUSCANY, 8" $250.00–275.00
VELMOSS SCROLL, 11½" $325.00–375.00
Row 4:
CHLORON, 10½" $300.00–350.00
MAYFAIR, 8",
corner pocket, #1014–8 ....$200.00–250.00
MOSTIQUE, 10½" $250.00–300.00
Row 5:
WHITE ROSE, 6½", #1288–6 ....$225.00–275.00
CAPRI trial glaze, 5", #1013–5, with series of code numbers
denoting trial glaze, rare $500.00–600.00
LOTUS, 7½", #L8–7 ....$300.00–350.00
WINCRAFT, 8½", #266–4 ....$200.00–225.00
COSMOS, 6½", #1285 ....$250.00–275.00

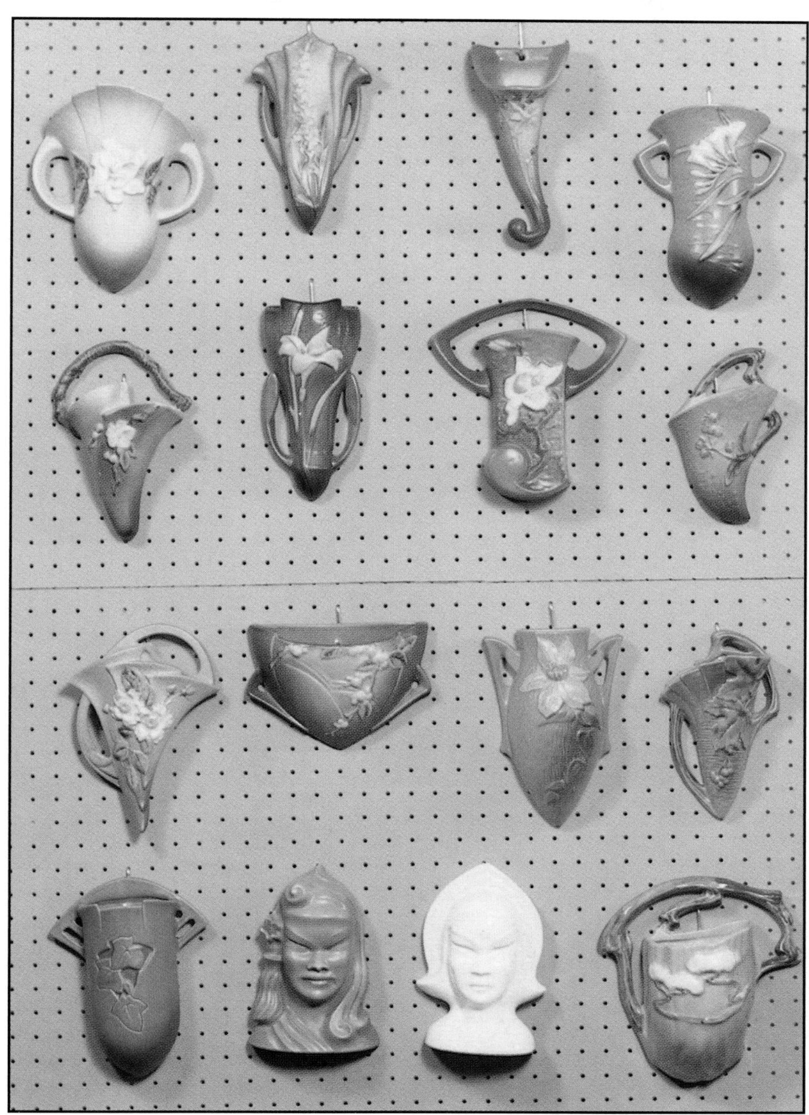

Plate 234

Wall Pockets

Plate 234

Row 1:

GARDENIA, 9½", #666–8 ....$300.00–350.00
FOXGLOVE, 8", #1292–8....................................$375.00–425.00
COLUMBINE, 8½", #1290–8 ....$500.00–600.00
FREESIA, 8½", #1296–8......................................$200.00–250.00

Row 2:

APPLE BLOSSOM, 8½", #366–8 ....$250.00–300.00
ZEPHYR LILY, 8", #1297–8, this example is marked under the glaze with the # series denoting trial and was the prototype original................................NPA
standard glazes...$225.00–275.00
MAGNOLIA, 8½", #1294 ....$225.00–275.00
BITTERSWEET, 7½", #866–7 ....$225.00–275.00

Row 3:

WHITE ROSE, 8½", #1289–8...............................$300.00–350.00
SNOWBERRY, 8", #1WP–8...................................$200.00–225.00
CLEMATIS, 8½", #1295–8...................................$200.00–225.00
BUSHBERRY, 8", #1291–8, orange.......................$300.00–350.00
blue...$400.00–450.00
green $350.00–400.00

Row 4:

SILHOUETTE, 8", #766–8 ....$225.00–275.00
BURMESE, 7½", #72–B, green glaze $200.00–250.00
BURMESE, 7½", #82–B, white glaze $200.00–250.00
MING TREE, 8½", #566–8...................................$325.00–375.00

Plate 235

Trials, Experimentals

Plate 235

"Serra," 6" $450.00–500.00
Pine Cone, 9", notation: "Bought at Chicago World's Fair, 1932" $900.00–1,000.00
Vase, 9", experimental $3,000.00–4,000.00
Mock Orange, 8", #974–8 .... $550.00–600.00
Decorated Imperial II, 5" $950.00–1,000.00

Experimentals

Plate 236

Row 1:
Freesia design, 9", blue background, yellow flowers $4,500.00–5,500.00
Gladiola design, inscribed on back: "GLADIOLUS"; green with white flowers $4,500.00–5,500.00
Lupines design, inscribed on back: "Pure White, White and Blue, Blue and Pink" $4,500.00–5,500.00

Row 2:
Black Eyed Susan: "yellow petals, center disk brown," blue background $3,500.00–4,000.00
Orchid, dark green background, white orchids $6,500.00–7,500.00
Blackberry, artist signed FAB, shaded green background $6,500.00–7,500.00

Row 3:
White Rose design, pink to blue with yellow rose $4,500.00–5,500.00
Bittersweet, incised on back: "Open shells, yellow orange, berries red, leaves green," blue background $4,500.00–5,500.00
Geranium, tan to green with pink flowers $4,500.00–5,500.00

Row 4:
Arrowhead design, inscription: "Flowers — white, leaves — green, flower centers — orange, buds — yellow green with white edges," blue background $3,500.00–4,000.00
Arrowhead design, inscription: "Flowers — white, leaves — green," pink to blue background $4,500.00–5,500.00
Larkspur design, inscription: "White, pink, blue, lavender, salmon (centers yellow)," blue background $4,500.00–5,500.00

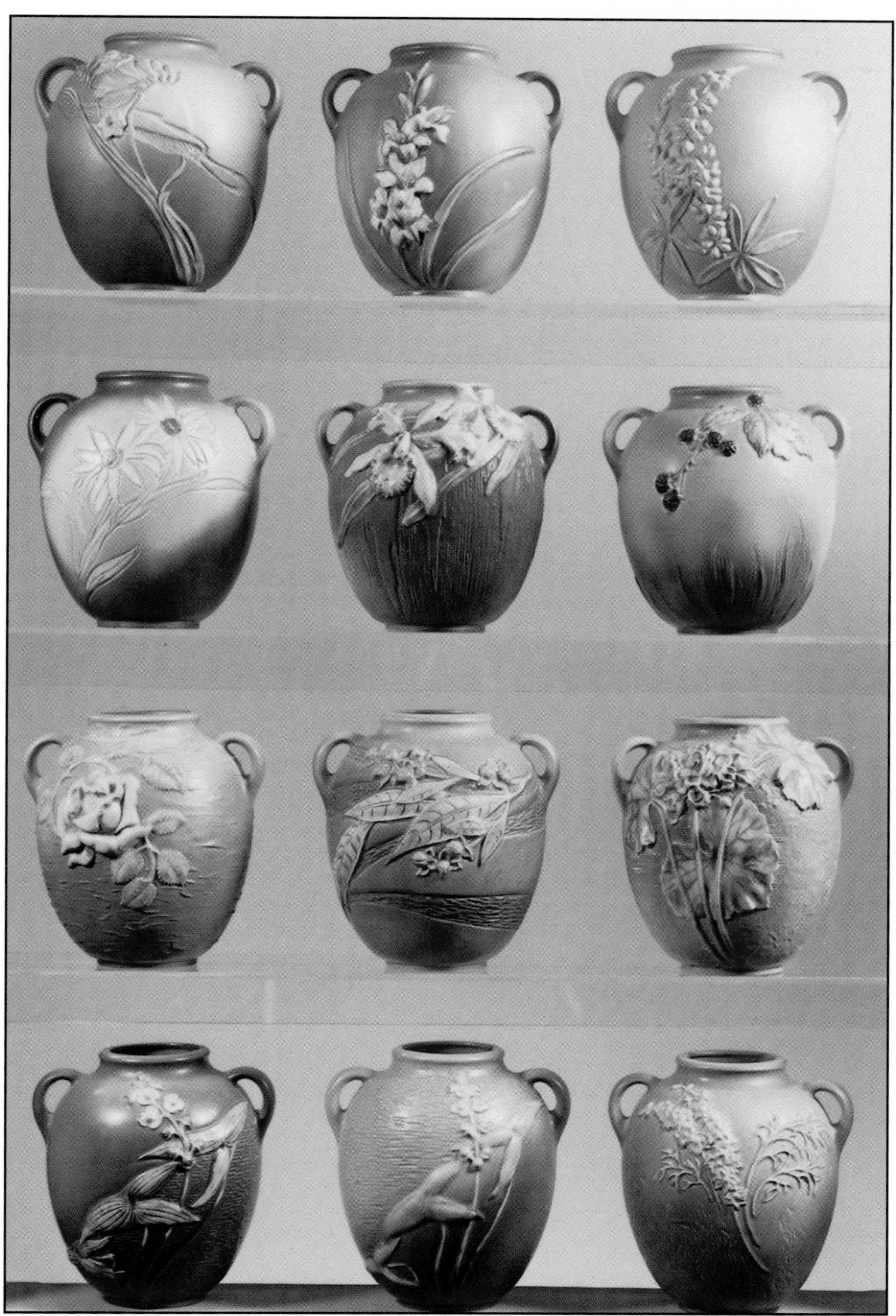

Plate 236

Plate 237

Experimentals

Plate 237

Row 1:

Pine Cone design, 6" $3,000.00–3,500.00

Pine Cone design, 8" $3,000.00–3,500.00

Vase, 5"..$1,750.00–2,000.00

Row 2:

Nude, 10", Panel type $6,500.00–7,500.00

Nude, 10" $2,500.00–3,250.00

Row 2 (continued):

Nude, 10" $7,500.00–8,500.00

Row 3:

Nude, 12½" $6,500.00–7,500.00

Pine Cone design, 20½" $7,500.00–8,500.00

Dogwood design, 16½",
decorated over Vista blank $7,500.00–8,500.00

Plate 238

Experimentals

Plate 238

Row 1:

Primrose design, 10" $5,000.00–6,000.00

Sweet Syringa or Mock Orange, 8½" $4,000.00–5,000.00

Floral design, 8"..............................$2,500.00–3,000.00

Floral design, 10",...........................$3,500.00–4,500.00

Row 2:

Gladiola design, 9½" $2,500.00–3,000.00

Bittersweet design, 13", shown in greenware, notation on base: Fruit, yellow, orange; Leaves, rich green; Flowers, white, yellow centers $1,500.00–1,750.00

Arrowhead design, 13", also in greenware, same colors indicated on base $1,500.00–1,750.00

Freesia design, 8½" $2,500.00–3,000.00

Trials, Experimentals

Plate 239

Row 1:

8" Plates, each with series of numbers representing color codes, each $700.00–800.00

Row 2:

Planter, 3", Roseville in relief, #s indicate trial glaze, ...$200.00–250.00

MING TREE, 8", in salmon pink with greenery $750.00–850.00

Window Box, 3½" x 10", tan to green $300.00–350.00

Row 3:

LAUREL, 8" $1,000.00–1,200.00

WILD ROSE, 10".............................$3,500.00–4,500.00

Vase, 8½" $475.00–550.00

MODERNE, 8", #796-8 ....$1,000.00–1,200.00

Plate 239

Plate 240

Trials, Experimentals

Plate 240

Row 1 (Trials):

- Tulip Vase, 6", #1001–6 .... $400.00–450.00
- Savona, 6" $550.00–600.00
- Baneda, 6" $1,000.00–1,200.00
- "New Colors" incised on base, 7" $350.00–400.00
- Cherry Blossom Bowl, 4" $1,250.00–1,500.00

Row 2 (Trials):

- Morning Glory, 8", textured background $1,200.00–1,450.00
- Morning Glory $1,200.00–1,450.00
- Morning Glory $1,200.00–1,450.00

Row 3 (Experimentals):

- Cherry Blossom, 7" $3,500.00–4,000.00
- Cosmos over Teasel blank, 8", #884 .... $2,500.00–3,000.00
- Freesia design, 7" $2,500.00–3,000.00
- Stylized Honeysuckle, 6½" $1,500.00–2,000.00

Row 4 (Experimentals):

- Floral design, 8" $5,000.00–6,000.00
- Wild Grape design, 9½" $4,000.00–4,500.00
- Cherry Blossom design, 7" $5,000.00–6,000.00

Plate 241
VICTORIAN ART POTTERY shape,
Vase, 11", rare motif with
ship on open seas $4,500.00–5,000.00

Plate 241

Plate 242

Trials, Experimentals

Plate 242
These trial glaze plates, left and right, measure 9½", and were from George Krause's estate. The Blackberry plate in the center is an experimental and is dated 11/19/63. A company letter in the Roseville files discusses the possibility of using some of the more popular older patterns as a basis for a dinnerware line; Blackberry was specifically suggested.
Color plates, each $450.00–500.00
Blackberry plate $1,500.00–2,000.00

Lamps

Plate 243
Base, 11½", marked
with series of #s...................................$400.00–500.00
IMPERIAL II, 5",
paper sticker...................................$1,000.00–1,250.00
Base, 12" $900.00–1,000.00
Base, 8½" $450.00–550.00

Plate 243

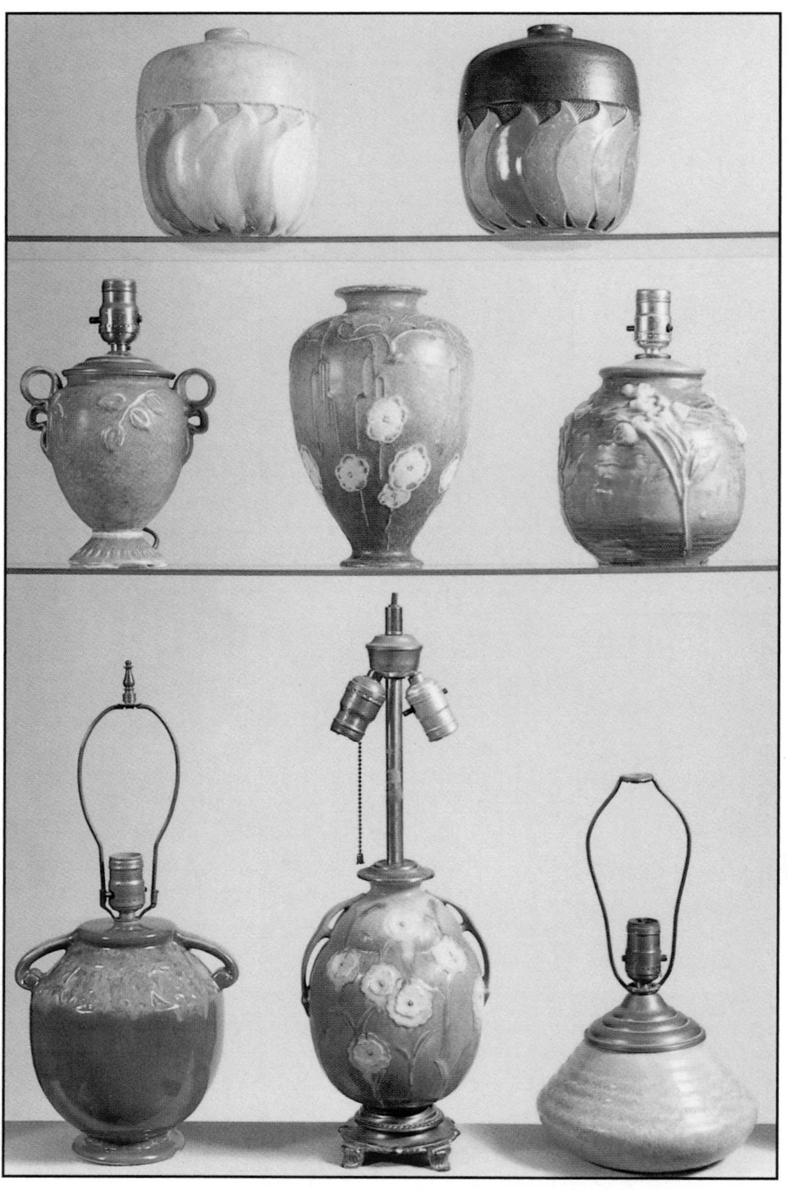

Plate 244

Lamps

Plate 244

Row 1:

IMPERIAL II Base, 8", #34–4 ....$900.00–1,000.00

IMPERIAL II Base, 8", sticker, #F39–4 ....$900.00–1,000.00

Row 2:

Base, 7", not Roseville

Base, 10", foil sticker, #F84–R7 ....$1,250.00–1,500.00

IXIA Base, 7½" $700.00–800.00

Row 3:

Base, 8½", not Roseville

Base, 10½" $1,250.00–1,500.00

Base, 5½", sticker $650.00–750.00

Radiator Cover

Plate 245

One of a set of radiator covers from the home of Russell T. Young, son of the founder of the Roseville Pottery, George Young. The design was by Frank Ferrell; George Krause made the tile. NPA.

Plate 245

Plate 246

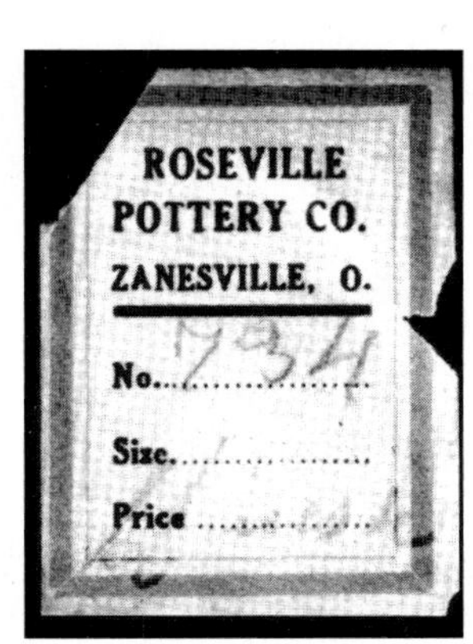

Plate 247

Umbrella Stands

Plate 246

BLENDED Basketweave, 21", marked with small paper label shown above $250.00–350.00

#701 BLENDED, 22" $250.00–350.00

#734 BLENDED, 21", marked with large paper label shown above $250.00–350.00

Plate 247

#132 BLENDED, 21½" $400.00–500.00

#705 BLENDED Stork, 19" $375.00–450.00

#719 BLENDED, 22" $400.00–450.00

Plate 248

Jardinieres and Pedestals

Plate 248
#126 BLENDED,
29½"...............................$350.00–400.00
MATT GREEN,
36"............................$4,000.00–4,500.00
DECORATED CREAMWARE,
29"................................$650.00–7500.00

Jardinieres and Pedestals

Plate 249
IVORY FLORENTINE,
29" $1,000.00–1,250.00
IVORY CAMEO, 34", Jard,
#439..................$1,500.00–2,000.00
ROZANE 1917, 28½" ...$950.00–1,050.00

Plate 249

Plate 250

Jardinieres and Pedestals, Umbrella Stand

Plate 250
DECORATED LANDSCAPE,
43" $4,000.00–5,000.00
Umbrella Stand with sgraffito and
squeezebag, 22".................$2,500.00–3,000.00
DECORATED LANDSCAPE,
44" $4,000.00–5,000.00

Jardinieres and Pedestals

Plate 251
#451 BLENDED
Iris, 31"......................................$650.00–750.00
#441 BLENDED, 38".........................$700.00–800.00
#414 BLENDED, 28".........................$600.00–700.00

Plate 251

Plate 252

Plate 253

Umbrella Stands

Plate 252
Gold and Silver
Decorated, 22½" $1,250.00–1,500.00
DECORATED MATT, 20", #724,
(artist's cipher unknown).....................$6,000.00–7,000.00
Gold and Silver
Decorated, 21½" $1,250.00–1,500.00

Jardinieres and Pedestals

Plate 253
Early CERAMIC, 49", Owens Pottery
FLEUR DE LIS, 20½", Jard, #412.....................$500.00–600.00

Plate 254

Umbrella Stands

Plate 254

NORMANDY, 20" $850.00–950.00
TOURIST, 22½" $6,000.00–7,000.00
CORINTHIAN, 20" $750.00–800.00

Jardinieres and Pedestals

Plate 255

DONATELLO, 34" $1,500.00–1,750.00
ROSECRAFT VINTAGE,
30½" $1,250.00–1,500.00
CORINTHIAN, 30½" $1,200.00–1,400.00

Plate 255

Plate 256

Sand Jars, Urn, Umbrella Stand

Plate 256

IVORY II, Sand Jar, 14½" $300.00–400.00
IVORY FLORENTINE,
Urn, 16½", #297 ....$400.00–500.00
IVORY FLORENTINE,
Umbrella, 18½", #298................$350.00–450.00
NORMANDY, Sand Jar,
14" $850.00–950.00

Plate 257

Jardinieres and Pedestals

Plate 257

DECORATED CREAMWARE with
Rose decal, 26" $850.00–1,000.00
ROZANE, 28", #516
on pedestal $1,250.00–1,500.00
FLORENTINE, 25" $800.00–1,000.00
WISTERIA, 24½" $2,000.00–2,500.00
blue $3,000.00–3,500.00

Rozane Floor Vases

Plate 258

Vase, 25", #850–3
(W Myers '02) $3,000.00–3,500.00
Vase, 29½",
(Mitchell) $4,000.00–5,000.00
Vase, 20", #632
(L McGrath) $2,500.00–3,000.00

Plate 258

Plate 259

Jardinieres and Pedestals

Plate 259

- DONATELLO, 23½"........................$800.00–1,000.00
- ARTCRAFT, 24½"......................$1,750.00–2,000.00
- CHERRY BLOSSOM, 25½",
  - brown....................$2,000.00–2,500.00
  - pink.......................$3,000.00–3,500.00
- CORINTHIAN, 24".............$750.00–850.00

Jardinieres and Pedestals

Plate 260

- ARTCRAFT, 28"....................$3,500.00–4,000.00
- BLACKBERRY, 28"..............$3,500.00–4,000.00
- DAHLROSE, 30½"...............$1,250.00–1,500.00

Plate 260

Plate 261

Jardinieres and Pedestals

Plate 261

DOGWOOD II, 30" $1,250.00–1,500.00
ROZANE 1917, 35" $1,250.00–1,500.00
VISTA, 28" $3,500.00–4,500.00

Jardinieres and Pedestals

Plate 262

JONQUIL, 29" $2,500.00–3,000.00
NORMANDY, 28" $1,200.00–1,400.00
SUNFLOWER, 29" $3,500.00–4,500.00

Plate 262

Plate 263

Umbrella Stand, Jardinieres and Pedestals

Plate 263

#720 MATT GREEN,
23"................................$1,250.00–1,500.00

PEONY, 30",
#661 on jard. $1,500.00–1,750.00

BLENDED MOSTIQUE,
27½" $350.00–400.00

Umbrella Stands

Plate 264

#727 BLENDED,
20" $250.00–350.00

EARLAM, 20", foil sticker,
#741 . . . . $2,500.00–3,000.00

#609 BLENDED,
20" $275.00–375.00

Plate 264

Plate 265

Jardinieres and Pedestals

Plate 265
FOXGLOVE, 30½", #659 on jardiniere
green/pink $1,750.00–2,000.00
blue $1,500.00–1,750.00
pink $1,250.00–1,500.00
ROSECRAFT BLENDED, 28",
no mark $900.00–1,000.00

Plate 266

Jardinieres and Pedestals

Plate 266
SNOWBERRY, 25", #1P8 U.S.A. on ped; #1J8 on jard....................$800.00–900.00
LUFFA, 24½"....................$1,250.00–1,500.00
LA ROSE, 24½"....................$800.00–900.00
ZEPHYR LILY, 25", #671–8, blue....................$900.00–1,000.00
brown $750.00–850.00
green....................$650.00–750.00

Plate 267

Assorted Floor Pieces

Plate 267

EARLAM Sand Jar, 12½" $1,500.00–1,750.00
CARNELIAN I Floor Vase, 18½" $500.00–600.00
MING TREE Floor Vase, 15½", #586–15 .... $550.00–650.00
#708 BLENDED Umbrella Stand, 19½" $350.00–450.00
FLORANE (Late Line) Sand Jar, 12", #52–12 .... $100.00–150.00

Plate 268

Umbrella Stands

Plate 268

BUSHBERRY, 20½", #779–20
- blue $1,500.00–1,750.00
- green $1,000.00–1,100.00
- orange $800.00–900.00

SUNFLOWER, 20½",
paper sticker $5,000.00–6,000.00
DOGWOOD I, 19½" $900.00–1,000.00

Autumn Jars

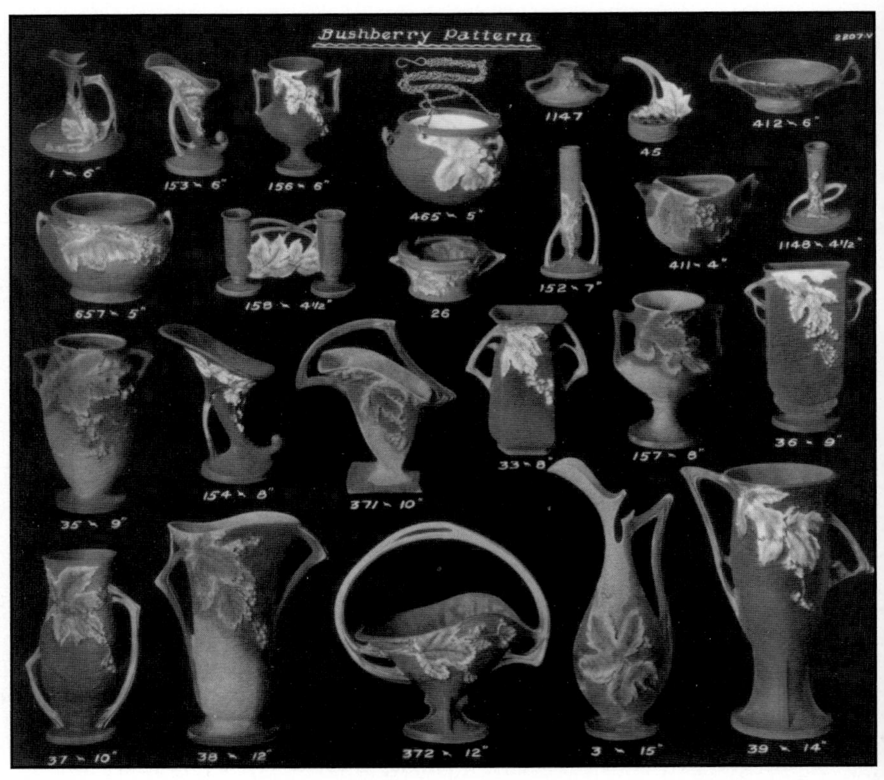

Bushberry

Cosmos

Donatello

Donatello

Ferella

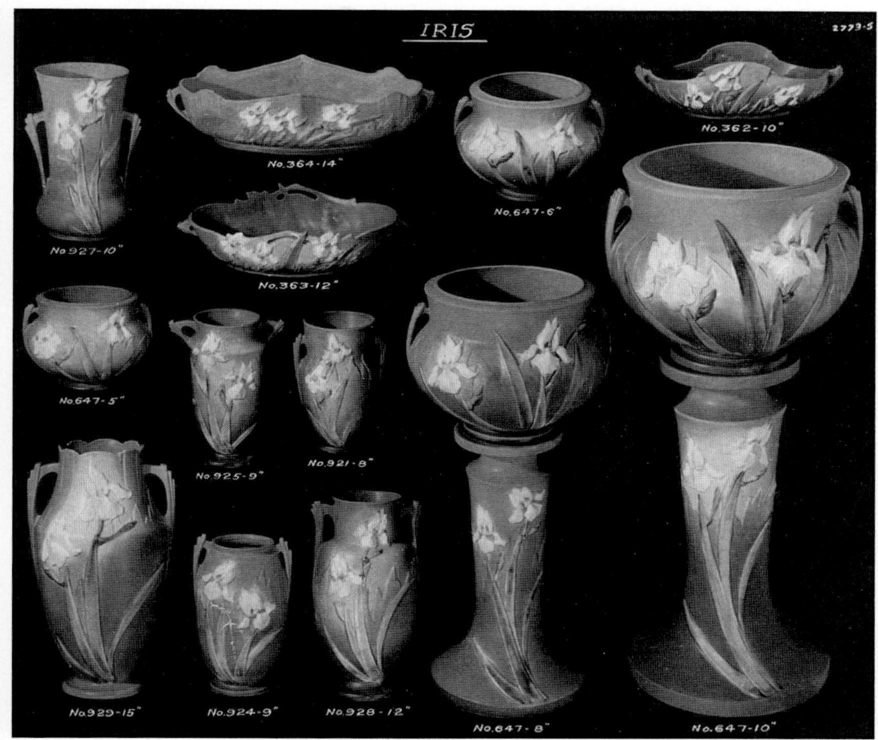
IRIS
No.364-14"
No.362-10"
No.647-6"
No.927-10"
No.363-12"
No.647-5"
No.925-9"
No.921-8"
No.929-15"
No.924-9"
No.928-12"
No.647-8"
No.647-10"

Iris

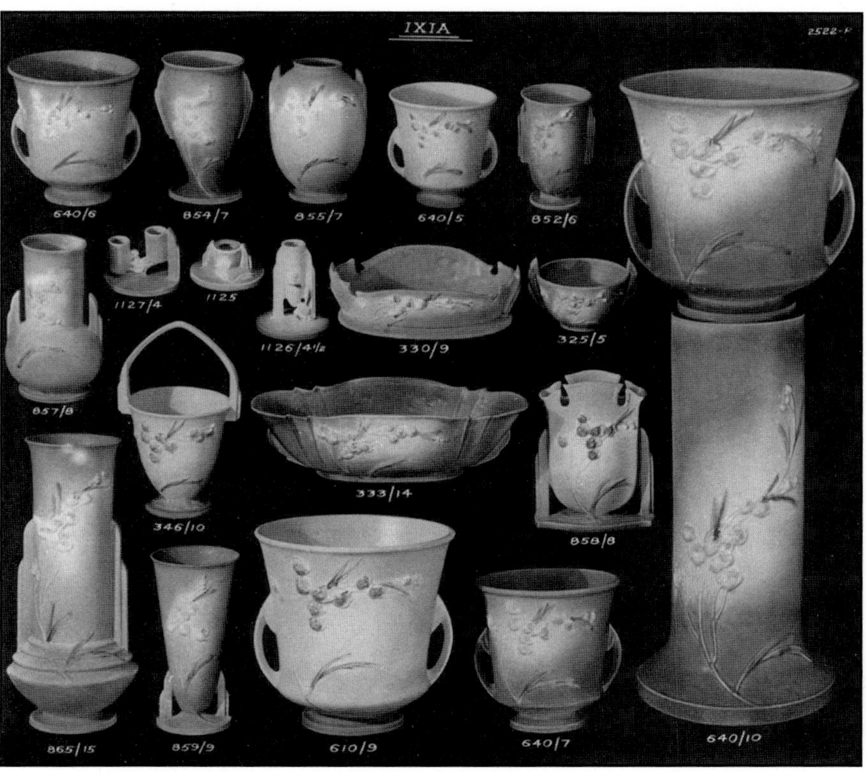
IXIA
640/6
854/7
855/7
640/5
852/6
1127/4
1125
1126/4½
330/9
325/5
857/8
346/10
333/14
858/8
865/15
859/9
610/9
640/7
640/10

Ixia

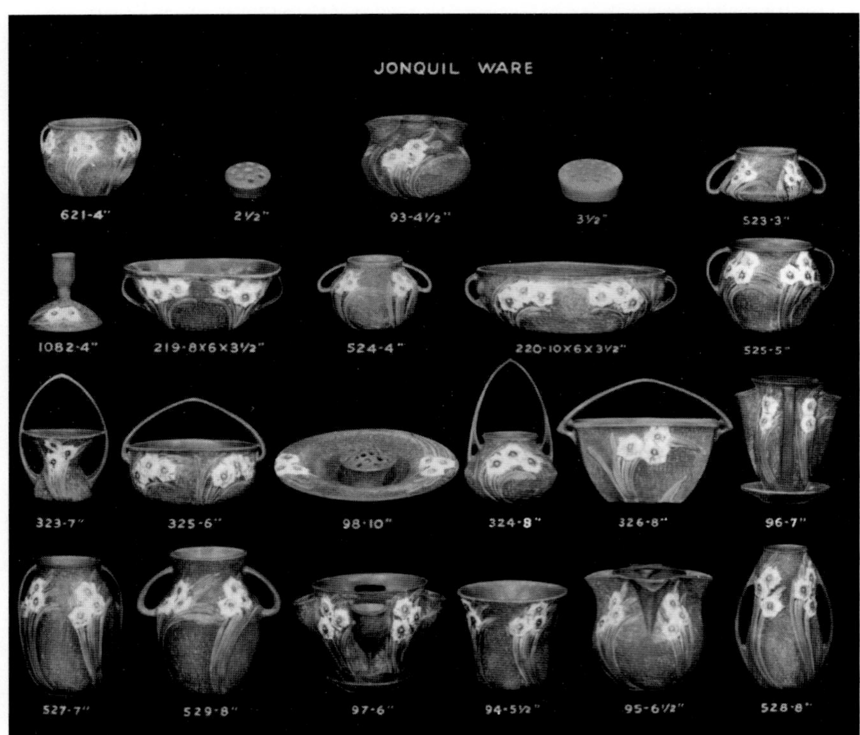

Jonquil

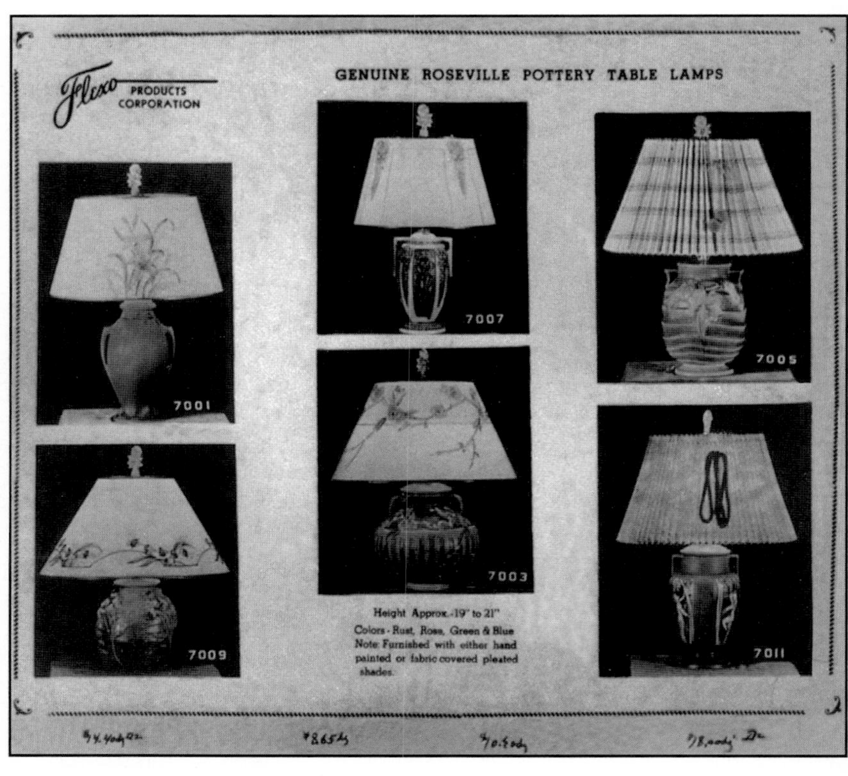

Lamps

Lamps

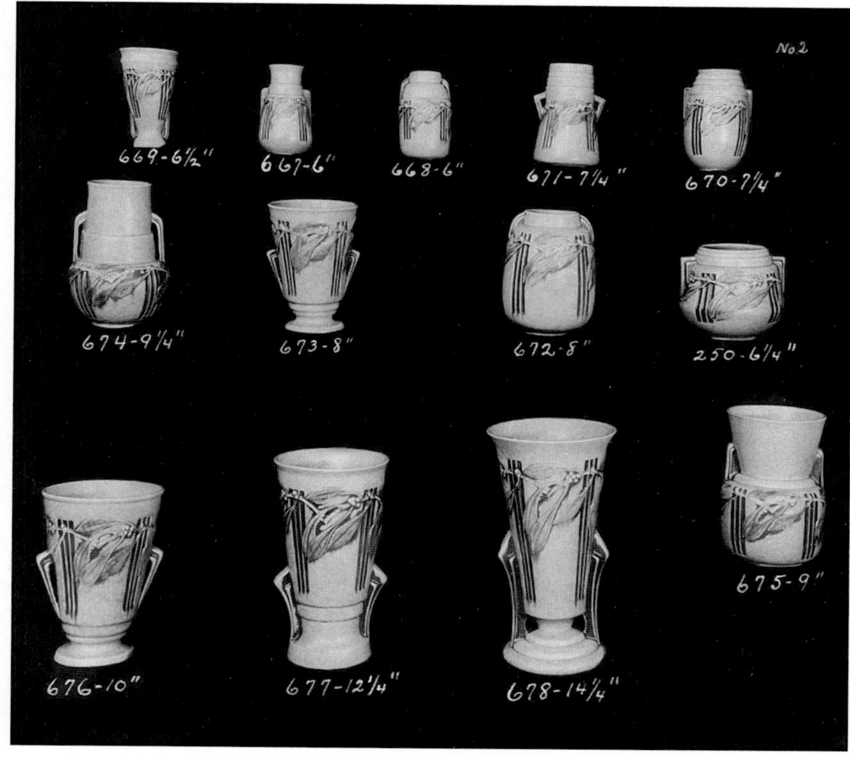

Laurel

Montacello

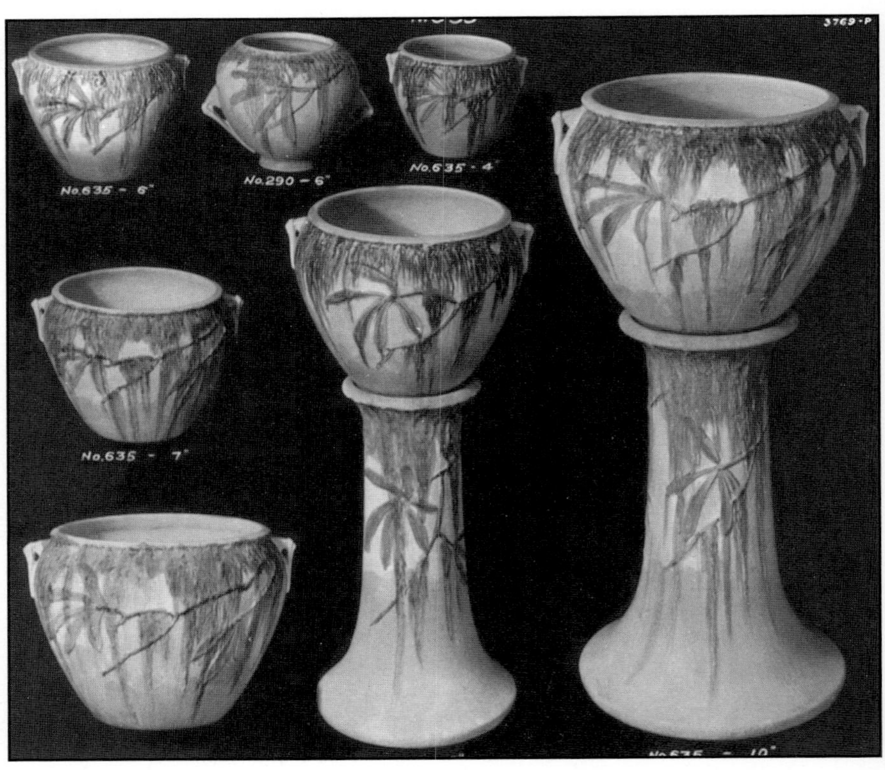

Moss

Mostique

Mostique

Persian

Pine Cone

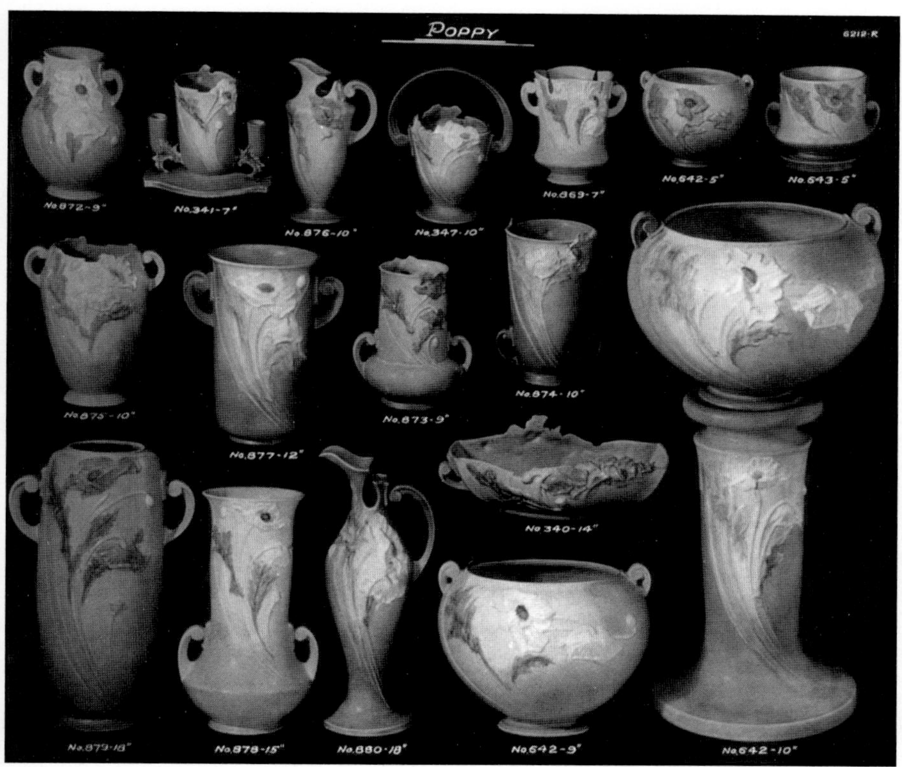
POPPY
6212-R
No.872-9"
No.341-7"
No.876-10"
No.347-10"
No.869-7"
No.642-5"
No.643-5"
No.875-10"
No.877-12"
No.873-9"
No.874-10"
No 340-14"
No.879-18"
No.878-15"
No.880-18"
No.642-9"
No.642-10"

Poppy

POPPY
6213-R
No.642-4"
No.334-4"
No.1130-5"
No.1129"
No.35"
No.358-5"
No.870-8"
No.867-6"
No.336-5"
No.1281-8"
No.871-8"
No.866-6"
No.868-7"
No.338-10"
No.339-12"
No.337-8"
No.348-12"
No.335-6"
No.642-6"
No.642-7"
No.642-8

Poppy

Thorn Apple

Thorn Apple

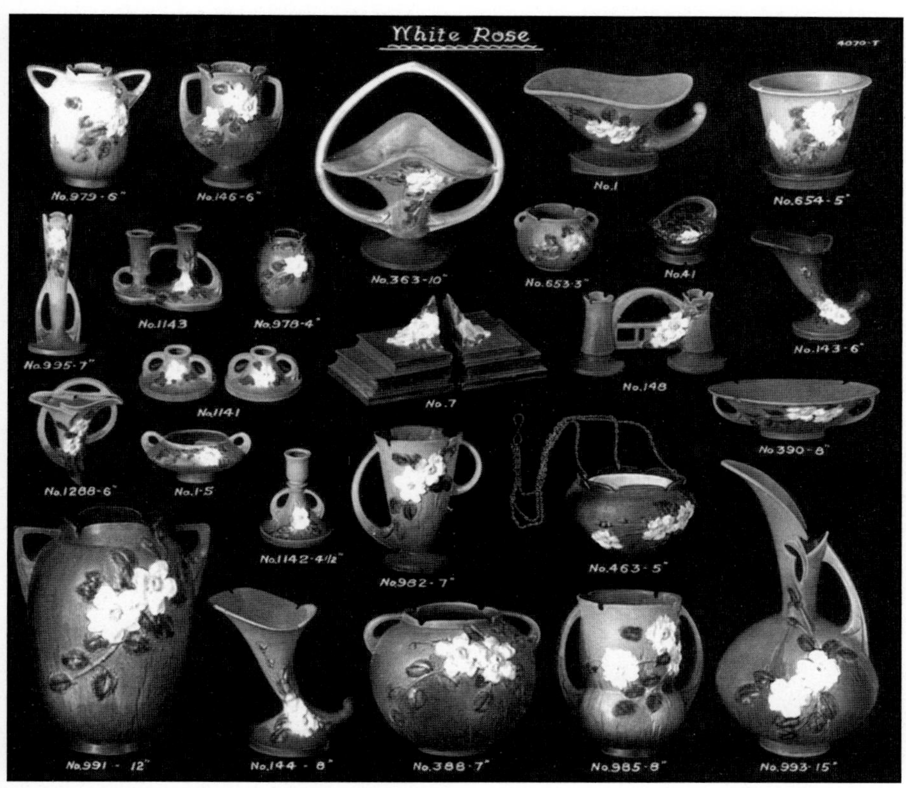

White Rose

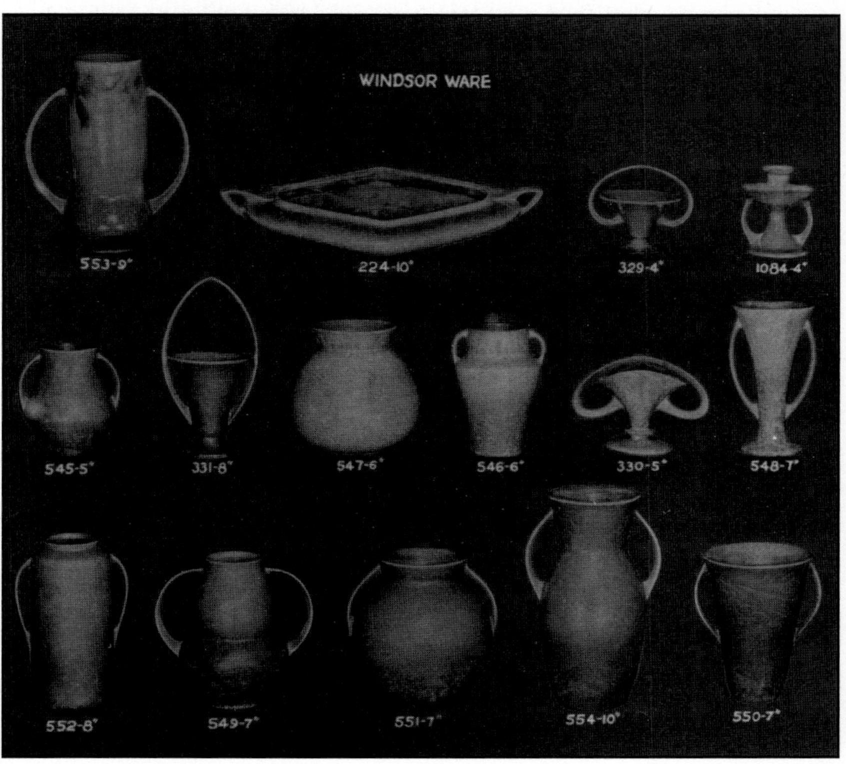

Windsor Ware

Bibliography

Alexander, Donald E. *Roseville Pottery for Collectors,* published by the author, 1970.

Bassett, Mark. *Introducing Roseville Pottery,* Schiffer Publishing Ltd., 1999.

Hall, Foster and Gladys. *Halls Pricing Formulas,* published by the authors, continually updated.

Ohio Historical Society. Roseville catalogs from their files.

Pauleo Pottery, Roseville Company booklet, 1914.

Schneider, Norris. "Blue Avenue Man and Wife Foremost Authorities on Roseville Pottery," *The Times Recorder,* March 31, 1968.

The Story of Rozane. Roseville Pottery Company booklet.

1905 Rozane Ware Catalog, Roseville Company.

1906 Rozane Ware Catalog, Roseville Company.

1916 Price Listing, Roseville Company.

Index

Numbers indicate pages in the Color Album of Pottery; catalog reprints are noted within brackets.